Living the Liturgy

MARILYN GUSTIN

LIVING THE LITURGY

LIGUORI
PUBLICATIONS

One Liguori Drive
Liguori, MO 63057-9999
(314) 464-2500

Imprimi Potest:
James Shea, C.SS.R.
Provincial, St. Louis Province
The Redemptorists

Imprimatur:
+ Edward J. O'Donnell, D.D.
Archdiocesan Administrator, Archdiocese of St. Louis

ISBN 0-89243-579-8
Library of Congress Catalog Card Number: 93-79676

Cover design by Myra Buechting

CONTENTS

The material in this book was first published in a slightly different form as a series of articles in *Liguorian* magazine.

Introduction

We are Catholics. If our faith and spiritual life are alive, the sacred liturgy of the Mass is central to our Christian experience. Our awareness of the presence of God revolves around our regular participation in the liturgy. Jesus said that whoever receives his blood and body is in union with him. (See John 6:56.) This is what we seek.

Too often we do not *experience* our union with Christ, even at Communion. We may wonder why we sometimes find the Mass less meaningful than we want it to be. We may feel puzzled. We may worry that "something is wrong with me," or we may blame the style of the liturgy. Deep in our hearts, we would like to experience the fullness of the Mass and be consciously aware of the presence of God.

Living the Liturgy is an invitation to focus on the Mass. We will explore ways to enter the liturgy more fully, experiencing its essence and its central place in our life in relationship with Christ—our spiritual life. In short, we will examine ways to help ourselves "get the most" out of the Mass.

CHAPTER ONE

Awakening a Sense of the Sacred

Our first step in deepening our experience of the spiritual journey of the Mass is to examine a wide inner experience too often missing from our participation in the liturgy: awareness of the sacred.

Years ago, not yet a Catholic, I entered an empty Catholic church. In the dim light, a feeling of mystery came over me. It seemed to me as if the very pews were reverent. As I walked silently forward toward the small red flame, I felt enveloped by a sacred presence.

I have been Catholic for nearly twenty years now. As everyone knows, much has changed in our churches. Many who knew the pre-Vatican II Church bewail the "loss of mystery" in the churches and in the Mass. Some blame it on the physical changes in the church, others on the liturgical changes.

That blame is misplaced. Outer conditions do not create the awareness of sacred mystery. A church is just as sacred as it ever was. Only our inner conditions can create or destroy the sense of the sacred. If something has changed, it is we ourselves.

What has happened to cause us to lose—or nearly lose—our inner awareness of sacredness?

The biggest influence on our attitudes and awareness has probably been societal conditioning. We live in a secular society where nothing is acknowledged to be sacred and holy, and reverence is offered to nothing. We participate actively in the secular society. Too often we accept the views and values of the media, and even those of us who remember a sacred space called church have lost our alertness to it.

When I worked at a retreat house, a retreatant came who was just out of prison. One of our buildings had been a convent filled with prayer for many years and was now open to visitors. As I took him to his room, he stopped just inside the door and demanded, "What *is* this place?" Even this man, who had not participated in church for years but who was inwardly alert, could *feel* the sacredness of this place.

The purpose of liturgy, the purpose of church buildings, is to bring God and us together; that is a sacred intent. If our attitudes are profane and mechanical, however, we can miss the sacred in the very place where it is strongest. It's a matter of being open and aware.

Reflections on Sacredness

What is your own most vivid experience of sacredness? We can revive our awareness by recalling times when we knew intuitively and forcefully that a place was sacred, where we could perceive God.

If you think sacredness is far from your current experience, reflect a few moments on the following questions:

- Doesn't it make a difference in *your* experience when a priest handles the chalice with reverence? That difference is awareness of the sacred.
- When a person walks across the sanctuary, can you tell if he or she is aware of the holiness of that space?

- Have you ever caught your breath at the sheer beauty of a church? a window? a flower?
- Has another person's devotion brought sudden humility to your heart? Your recognition of it is a response to sacredness.

We can honor sacredness wherever we find it in our memory or in our present experiences. Sacredness deserves our acknowledgment, our respect, our appreciation, our reverence. Reverence in the presence of the sacred gives honor to God, who creates the sacredness. Reverence for even a single sacred moment opens our hearts to what God wants to give us through the perception of that moment.

Conscious Preparation for the Sacred

Every time we go to Mass, we may encounter the sacred presence of the Lord—if we are open to it through awareness. God rarely pounds down our resistances. If we want to meet the Lord in the Mass *and know it*, we will consciously prepare ourselves.

The Church asks us to avoid food for one hour before Mass. So little! Because it is so little, do we ignore it? After all, what is it for? The intention of that one-hour fast is to remind us of the sacredness of what we are about to do. It is preparation time.

However, fasting may not have the desired effect for many of us. We are more likely to renew our sense of the sacred and open our hearts to participation in it if we take that hour of fast and enrich it.

We can make it a quiet time, relaxing a little and center ourselves. Turn off the TV, sit down, wait quietly, breathe deeply. We can offer this time and ourselves to the Lord in prayer. We can look ahead to the day's readings and recall the sacred place we are about to enter and the sacred action we will share. Thus, we predispose ourselves to recognize the sacred in the familiar words and actions of the liturgy.

You may protest that you cannot do this because of family pressures. That may be true if your children are preschool age—although most parents are pretty inventive when something is important to them. If the kids are school age, try making this a family time and let the children participate. *Building Family Faith* by Lisa Bellecci-st.romain (Liguori Publications, 1993) gives activities and prayers for families keyed to the Sunday readings of all three liturgical cycles. Family members who do not wish to participate can be asked to be quiet or to go to another part of the house. Such unnecessary noise as the TV can be controlled by parents.

ENTERING THE SACRED SPACE

In the anticipation born of this quiet hour, we go to church ready to be attentive to its sacredness in place and in action. When Moses saw the burning bush that was not consumed (see Exodus 3:1-5), a voice told him to take off his shoes, for he was standing on holy ground. The removal of shoes is a gesture of reverence for the sacred in a sacred place.

I personally think that going into church unshod out of reverence is a good idea, but I doubt that the gesture means the same thing to most people! What *can* we do, then? First, we can dress well, choosing our clothes to match the sacredness and the spiritual intent of our action in the Mass. Don't we usually dress well to meet important people? Besides, what would be the effect if our priest celebrated Sunday Mass in *his* picnic shorts and T-shirt?

We can pause as we enter the church. Standing at the threshold, we can notice the altar, appreciate the flowers, feel affection for the people present. We can use the blessed water to signify our hoped-for unity with the sacred action about to occur.

Full perception of the sacred inspires silence, and silence helps us recognize the holy. Sacredness and silence belong together. So we can leave our chatter in the car. We can walk silently and reverently to our place. We can genuflect to the Blessed Sacrament with conscious intention, acknowledging that it is the Lord to whom we kneel.

We can pray silently in our own heart in those moments before Mass begins. Thus, we enter the sacred space, ready for sacred participation. One caution: if you follow these suggestions, remember that many others in the church will not be observing them. One of the best ways to destroy your own awareness of God's sacred presence is to criticize your neighbor in your heart.

God is present in the sacred space of the church and in the sacred acts of the liturgy. We can begin to become more fully aware of God by opening our hearts to sacredness, to the holy. Then the sacred will carry us into awareness of God.

In the sacred silence of the sacred church, then, let God see your heart just as it is. God is pure compassion, total love. Jesus repeatedly told his disciples not to be afraid, *because* he was present. In sacredness, there is only compassion—enough to arouse true awe and real humility in our heart. Divine love washes our feet and cradles our heart, if we allow it. It can happen during every liturgy, if we are open to it.

CHAPTER TWO

Sacred Symbol, Sacred Ceremony

When one becomes Catholic as an adult, everything is fresh and fascinating. To be sure, keeping it that way requires an effort of will, but I shall never forget the impact of the first Masses I saw. Their power for me did not come from knowledge, for I had little information about the Mass.

Moments still stand out in my memory: people genuflecting and kneeling before Mass began; the raised arms and open hands of the priest; the cruciform blessing of the water and wine; the elevation of the host. Of course, I had questions. Why the vestments? What did the various things on the altar signify? Did the gestures of the priest imply anything in particular?

Most of all, I wanted to know why these things touched my heart so strongly even though I did not understand them. Through an attention undimmed by habit, they communicated to me the presence of the Lord. How did that happen?

It happened because that is exactly what symbols do. They participate both in what they symbolize and in our own being. Sacred symbols, like sacredness in general, mediate between ourselves and the Lord. They *are* sacred, as the presence of God is sacred. Being physical, symbols can communicate meaning to us. In the Mass, every gesture, every action, every object is a sacred symbol, belonging by nature both to the realm of the divine and to our own daily realm.

The Nature of Symbols

In many minds, a symbol merely "stands for" something else. If we say, "It's only a symbol," we may mean it only points to something else. If this is what you think a symbol is, you may have difficultly with the real meaning of this chapter. A symbol is not a substitute for "the real thing."

A symbol is a form (a word, a gesture, an action, an object) which *by its own nature* participates in two levels of reality at once. Think about a valentine; it *is* paper, probably red. It belongs to the physical, inanimate world. Still, it makes an impact on the receiver: it affects the emotions, the mind. Feelings and thoughts are not physical; they belong to a different level of reality. A valentine thus participates in the physical world and in the emotional or mental world. It's a simple piece of paper, but that's not all it is.

All symbols are like that. They exist in two or more worlds at once and so mediate between them. This may well be a new way of thinking about symbols for you. If so, do try to keep it in mind so you can fully understand the rest of this chapter. It is an extremely important point, one that cannot be overemphasized.

The Mass powerfully mediates to us the presence of the Lord, because the Mass is made of sacred symbols. They communicate to us the reality of God, because they *participate in* that reality. Such mediated communication is vital to our spiritual life.

Sacred symbols are uniquely able to draw us beyond our mind, beyond our emotions, into spiritual participation. They *are* sacred, they *are* "spiritual," yet they are not exclusively of the spiritual realm. Sacred symbols are also familiar physical forms, so they link us to spiritual reality. One sacred symbol—the consecrated host—links us directly to God because it *is* both *truly* wheat and *truly* God. The reality of Christ has pervaded, taken possession of, the form of the wheat. Experiencing that real, spiritual link depends on our own attentiveness and receptivity.

The Quality of Attention

The richness of our experience of symbols depends partly on the quality of our attention and partly on information. If we want to experience the symbols of the Mass more deeply, we will attend to them with an open heart. Sacred symbols speak more forcefully to the heart than to the mind, as they did to my heart even before my mind was informed. This quality of attention can be learned.

First of all, we can really see and really hear what goes on at Mass. It *can* be fresh for us every time, if we *attend* and not just drift along half in a daydream. We can make an effort to be present with all of ourselves: mind, heart, spirit, and body, alert and consciously *in* the church—not with last night's movie or this afternoon's guests.

Second, attention means listening with our feelings and intuition of the heart. It's a little like listening to a child who doesn't speak clearly yet or "knowing" what a pet is trying to say to us. In intuitive attention, an inner openness occurs when the mind and body are quiet. It is a spiritual capacity and everybody has it, although it may be rusty from lack of exercise.

If we already seek the Spirit in our living every day, then the symbols of the Mass will be more alive for us when we attend to them. They will be God's communication to us, and we will consciously use them to communicate with God.

As our spiritual life grows, so will our appreciation of

symbols. Symbols will deepen our spiritual life, for they act directly on us. For the richest experience of sacred symbols, however, we also benefit from information about them (although a complete study of all the symbols would require more time and space than we have here.)

Let's consider a few of the most familiar symbols of the Mass, following our own steps as we go.

Blessed by Water and the Cross

When we enter the church, we make the Sign of the Cross over our body with blessed water. A discussion of the symbols of both cross and water could expand far beyond a paragraph. Here are a few hints, however.

The Sign of the Cross recalls Jesus' passion and resurrection—his glorification for our redemption. The cross suggests that all the things of heaven (the vertical bar) and all the things of earth (the horizontal bar) are joined at the center, which is Christ.

Because *we* make this sacred gesture, the symbol suggests our acceptance of redemption and our intention to join all our life to Christ, to participate in Christ's death and resurrection. In touching our head, heart, and shoulders, we are saying that our mind and emotions (head) and the center of our life (heart) and all our strength (shoulders) are given to the cross of Christ. Is it true for us, this lovely gesture?

The water directly recalls baptism, itself a powerful symbol of dying to old life and rising to transformed living. Moreover, water is necessary to life. It is humble, always accepting the forms of its container. Water is for cleansing. It is strong—it wears away rocks and softens everything it touches.

All that—and more—in one simple gesture? Such is the purpose and power of sacred symbols; they bring it all together in our awareness, without words or mental explanation.

Gestures as Symbol

After we bless ourselves, we go to our pew. Before entering, we genuflect to the Blessed Sacrament. Kneeling to another, suggests submission, acknowledgment of higher position and greater power, allegiance, reverence, and honor. In the West, we are prone to say that we kneel only to God. What does that mean to you? We attend to this symbol of devoted self-giving before we seat ourselves, because of the majesty of the One to whom we kneel. You may particularly wish to observe the other times in the Mass when we kneel. What does kneeling suggest to you at those times?

At several points in the Mass, we stand up. Standing is also symbolic. When we meet someone new, we stand out of respect for that person. In the Mass, we stand to pray, showing respect for God. Standing in the presence of another also suggests poise, readiness, strength, attention, and even the receiving of commands. What else does the gesture of standing suggest to you?

These acts are symbolic gestures that we ourselves perform. When we perform them attentively, they draw us into the presence of God. Even when performed automatically, they have a subtle effect—but their beauty and intensity will be enriched by our attention.

Priest as Symbol

While the priest also performs symbolic gestures and acts, he himself becomes a sacred symbol when he celebrates Mass.

He is one of us, so he symbolizes us—each of us and all of us as a community—when he prays to the Father on our behalf. He is like Christ when he recalls in action the Last Supper and the institution of the Eucharist. He is an intermediate; he participates in our reality and, by his office, in Christ's reality.

The priest wears special clothing to celebrate Mass. He vests because in the symbol of the Mass, his personality does not matter, only the office he holds. His individual quirks (while we may love him for them) are veiled by the vestments. In this way, our attention is focused on the astounding significance of his mediation between God and us, and we will be undistracted from the reality of the divine Presence.

Each individual vestment is a sacred symbol as well, intended partly as priestly prayer but also as wonderful symbols for us. The vestments suggest virtues that are perfected in Christ and that we (both priest and people) must continually strive to attain.

Symbolism of the Vestments

As you read the following information about the symbolism of each vestment, give yourself a few moments to ponder the meaning of these sacred symbols in your own heart.

First, the priest puts on the alb, a long white garment, usually linen, that covers the priest's body. Whiteness suggests purity of heart, single-minded focus on God, and innocence of motive. Linen is not naturally white; much washing and bleaching makes it so. Purity of heart is not easily attained!

Next comes the cincture, a cord tied around the waist. It symbolizes chastity, which requires a focused and concentrated mind. Chastity also predisposes one to deeper prayer. Chastity here means the right use of our sexuality, *according to our state in life.* Without conscious control of our powerful sexual energies and without a concentrated mind, the deepest prayer is not possible.

Then the priest places the stole over his shoulders. It

symbolizes the spiritual powers and dignity of the priestly office. It reminds us of his mediation between us and God. Traditionally, the stole also suggests the "robe of immortality"—the everlasting life we all desire.

The chasuble, the priest's outer garment, represents Christian love for God and neighbor and the service that expresses that love. The chasuble is the garment we all see. The others—purity of heart, chastity and concentration, and priestly powers to represent us and Christ—are mostly hidden. They are inner conditions, in the priest as well as in us. Love expressed in service is something we can experience directly, and so we see the chasuble.

The symbolic value of the vestments is not only for the priest alone. These symbols express essential qualities in Christian spiritual life. If we know their meaning, we can reflect on them as we participate in the Mass. We can look for hints in the Mass about developing these virtues in our own living.

Surrendering to God in Joy

Turning from the vestments to the priest's actions, we see that almost every gesture is potentially symbolic. The directives for saying Mass tend to preserve the symbols, sometimes with explanation. Anyone who is interested can learn their symbolism. I challenge you to discover them for yourself. Ask your priest about books that might help you.

The next time you participate in the Mass, you may wish to attend more with your heart to all the symbols. This chapter has only enough information to alert you and get you started. The power of symbols can draw you further. And in the Mass, "further" can only mean further into God.

In a certain sense, the whole Mass is a symbol. *Remember, this does not mean it stands for something other than itself.* It means that it *is* an event both in the spiritual realm and in our ordinary world. It effectively brings us into the kingdom we seek, where Christ is everything and we are Christ's.

In the Mass, attention is on God and the things of God; our emotions may be moved by the beauty of God, our minds may be enlightened by understanding God's purposes, our wills may be strengthened to do God's will, our hearts may be drawn deeper into the heart of God. Because it is all symbol in the most profound sense of that term, everything that happens at Mass—gesture, action, prayer, sacrifice, and the receiving of the Lord into ourselves—can synthesize within us what we want our spiritual life to be: surrendering to God in joy, loving God, and receiving God's full gift of himself.

CHAPTER THREE

The Mass Begins

Let's imagine that we have entered the church, made the Sign of the Cross, and genuflected to the Blessed Sacrament. We have been silent, but our silence has been filled with prayer. The Mass is about to begin.

First, we recall the sacred act and sacred gesture we are about to experience, the sacredness that is the foundation of the Mass. We recall the power of symbols to bring our whole being to God. Sacredness and symbols will follow us throughout our participation in the Mass. Even if we do not *think* about them, they are intrinsic to the sacred liturgy. Now, the priest enters, and with the gathered community, we begin the familiar introductory rites.

The Introductory Rites

During the first months as a Catholic, I lived at a retreat house and experienced the Mass in many situations. There were wedding Masses, funeral Masses, sunrise Mass, Midnight Mass, Masses for big celebrations such as Thanksgiving, even a picnic Mass—and, of course, daily Mass. I remember being struck by the steadiness evoked in me with the first words of the introductory rites. No matter what the situation—happy or sad, fun or solemn—there was always the invocation of the Lord's grace, the recognition God.

The Entrance Song

Each Mass, among its other riches, offers us a *particular* theme for reflection, learning, and practice. The entrance song announces this theme, which always aims to bring us closer to God through understanding and action. It invites us to focus on the particular part of our relationship with God that the Church offers today.

In the same way, our spiritual life proceeds by *particular* steps. It does not happen all at once. It is not vague. So we may take the theme for the Mass as our focus for inner growth this day or this week. It is a concrete possibility for right now.

The Greeting

The priest greets the community by offering us the grace, the peace, the love of the Lord. We respond by returning it to him. In this moment, all the people in the church are one in intention and one in the flow of divine grace. When we heartily wish grace for one another, it flows unhindered through all of us.

The greeting is a mutual reminder that everything we do here together is a sacred act, done in the name of the Holy Trinity. To the extent that we allow the words of the Mass to penetrate our social surface, this moment expresses the basic attitude of all members of the Christian community to one another. What more could we wish for one another than full mutual participation in the grace and love of God?

Few practices can help our spiritual life more dramatically than to activate this attitude in all our relationships. What if this week we said silently to every person we meet or see, "The grace and peace of the Lord be with you"? Try it and discover for yourself what happens.

The Penitential Rite

Now, reminded of the gracious love of God for us, we turn to penitence. The penitential rite may be the point in the Mass at which we become automatons. Penitence is genuinely comfortable for no one. Few of us examine our lives before every Mass; even if we do, we will not likely tell our neighbors about it. So it is easy to repeat the familiar words without consciously entering into them.

Yet without a penitent heart, we simply cannot have a relationship with God. Penitence and humility hold hands. If we imagine that we only come to the Lord when we are whole and accomplished, we delude ourselves, making a true relationship impossible. We know that intimacy with friends and family is based on truthfulness. Anything less creates falsity, hiddenness, manipulation, and self-righteousness. If we seek a closer relationship with the Lord, then, we must be humbly truthful with God, exactly as we are.

A fundamental recognition in Christianity is that we are not "together"; we feel scattered and wounded and messed up. We want to be better. The first step in moving toward God and our own betterment is acknowledging honestly where we are right now. The second step is turning around to face into the light of God's love. Those two acts are penitence. The invitation of the penitential rite is to confess our separation from God and ask God to bridge the gap with his forgiveness.

Penitence is hard on our ego-centered false selves. We'd prefer to believe only good things about ourselves. We'd prefer not to remember our imperfections and our brokenness. We like being self-sufficient. Since we tend to be so harsh with ourselves when we think something is wrong with us, we fear the judgment of God. Naturally, then, we may prefer to be "on automatic" when the Mass reminds us of our shadowed side.

People who have had near-death experiences (regaining consciousness after apparently dying) report something interesting about judgment. Their experiences seem consistent: they encounter a person of light or a light that is love. Facing into that beauty, they know they are totally loved, totally and unconditionally forgiven. Recognizing that love, they know themselves to be less beautiful than it is. And in that light, they judge themselves.

This is consistent with the penitential rite. In the light of the Lord's grace, just invoked and flowing in the gathered community, we see and acknowledge that we need forgiveness. We have judged ourselves. Now we freely open that judgment to God's action.

God always forgives. He never holds our sins against us. Once we have called on the Lord for love and mercy, our wrongs no longer matter at all. Just as brokenness is the truth about us, so this merciful, forgiving love is the truth about God. We could love penitence because it brings God's love more fully into our hearts.

If we enter mindfully and heartily into the penitential rite, we will become humble. Humility is not harshness with ourselves. It isn't even recognition of our sinfulness—by itself. Humility is recognizing the whole truth about ourselves and about God simultaneously, then living in that awareness of both.

We really can trust God to forgive. We need not be afraid of our own mistakes, confusions, bad intentions, or miserable habits. God will always grant mercy and peace—and the strength to go on, healed, if we cooperate.

Thus, we become humble because we are forgiven, receivers of God's ever-full stream of mercy. Because brokenness and forgiveness are true of every one of us, we confess to one another and pray for one another. The penitential rite of the Mass can enliven our humility over and over again.

To foster your spiritual awareness of God's loving forgiveness, try taking the penitential rite into your heart—and look around at your brothers and sisters when you admit your situation to them. Pray for the rest of the community, just as you request them to pray for you. Beg mercy for all of us together, as well as for yourself.

The Gloria

The most natural response to God's forgiveness (besides comfort and relief) is gratitude—thanksgiving that God has given love and mercy; praise that God is so splendid and so magnificent and so generous. So, of course, we pray the Gloria!

The Gloria first recalls the words of the angels to the shepherds on Christmas. (See Luke 2:14.) Then we praise God the Father and Jesus the Son, recalling Christ's powerful, redemptive work of forgiveness. We ascribe to Jesus the highest position, united with the Holy Spirit and the Father in the Trinity.

We praise the Lord because "you take away the sins of the world." When I first heard this, I thought it was patently untrue—the world is hardly free of sin! Eventually, with a little help from my friends, I came to understand it differently. It means that the Lord removes the sin of the world from our hearts and our lives, if we wish it.

The sense of separation from God that plagues us all is the root of that sin. We also consistently overemphasize the values of the rest of the world: possessions and possessing, getting everything we want, doing exactly as we please, comparing ourselves to others, taking care of "number one." Because we choose such attitudes, we continue to feel separate from God.

One earthly function of redemption in Christ is to take away these selfish qualities from our hearts and minds so we can be made fit for union with God. It is Jesus' goal for us. When the Son came as a human being, he "saved" all his disciples from the selfishness, the sinfulness, that keeps us away from oneness with God.

The Opening Prayer

Our last act in the introductory rites is the opening prayer. It is "proper," that is, specifically written for the particular day or season; therefore its words are different for each celebration. The opening prayer expresses the theme of the Mass in the form of prayer. This is not merely a sneaky way of reminding us of the day's theme, however. The theme is the focus for God's activity in our life for this day or week.

The opening prayer requests our loving God to make today's theme vital and effective in us. Prayers for such goodness are always answered, sometimes immediately. So we already begin to receive the benefits of *this* day's sacred celebration if we are receptive and attentive.

The Foundation of Our Spiritual Walk

We need only accept the gift and cooperate with the process of grace that redemption opens for us. The penitential rite and the Gloria, taken together, express the foundation of our spiritual walk: one foot, so to speak, is our asking God for forgiveness and the other foot is praising God for his great goodness. If we take our cue from this part of the Mass and make these two attitudes a daily, even hourly practice, our spiritual life will expand dramatically.

For a start, ten minutes every evening could be devoted to reviewing the day, seeking forgiveness where needed, then praising God in our heart. If we need words, we can use the Gloria—slowly, attentively, reflectively.

Both penitence and praise open our hearts to the love of God. Penitence allows us to receive God's gifts. Praise makes us more and more aware of the beauty of God and of the Lord's compassion to all. We cannot help but love God more when we praise him more. Praise opens our hearts to receive more of God's grace inside.

Loving God and receiving his gifts will eventually bring us home to union with the Trinity.

Not a single word of the Mass is accidental or without significance. The introductory prayers we say are vital to our stance before God, both during Mass and in our whole spiritual life. Therefore, let's give the Mass the quality of attention which will help us right from the entrance song.

Attention is an essential practice for growing closer to God anyway. Why not take up that practice at Mass? Our experience of liturgy will be greatly freshened and enriched as it becomes more conscious. Our spiritual progress will continue far more steadily as we learn to attend more steadily.

The aim of liturgy is great beyond words to express it. It can be fulfilled in us only if we give ourselves to it each time as if it were totally new. Shall we try it?

CHAPTER FOUR

The Word of the Lord

In Chapter Three we saw how we begin the Mass by responding to God's grace and presence with penitence and praise, the foundation for a living relationship with God. These actions are renewed at every Mass. The very existence of sacred liturgy fosters our conscious life with God, with Jesus, right in our familiar daily life.

Scripture Readings

After the opening prayer, we sit down to listen to the Scripture readings. Here is another moment in the Mass when we may be tempted to daydream. We've been standing, now we settle down to sit—and in other areas of our lives, we often become passive when we sit (when we watch TV, for example). By recognizing this temptation, we can make a conscious effort to strengthen our attention.

Sitting to hear the Word of God can be quite different from passive sitting. It can be like listening to our favorite speaker, whom we expect to tell us something precious about our favorite subject. Maybe it can be a little like "sitting on the edge of our seat." We can sit quietly but alertly so the body does not distract us from total attention to the words of the

Bible. Moreover, sitting is the position of the learner, showing that we are ready to be taught by God's word. Biblical words are not titillating entertainment. They can become food to our hearts, nourishment for our spirits.

When we ask what the readings offer our spiritual life, we are really asking what the Scripture itself has to do with our spiritual life. Christian spirituality without a vivid relationship to the Scripture is hardly imaginable.

Scripture is the word of God for us. Theologians expand on what that means, but let me simply share what "Word of God" means to me. If it is different for you, you can use these thoughts as a springboard for your own reflection.

The chief quality of God is self-communication in love. God wants to communicate with us so that we can enter fully into loving relationship with him. That's our spiritual life.

God has chosen to communicate with us in every imaginable way. He sent Jesus his Son; he created the beauty of our natural world; he created us to *want* to live in love with other people. And God inspired writers across the centuries to write the books of the Bible.

God is active in human life, and we can discern God's action through the history and ideas recorded in the Bible. If we want to know how God acts—or might act—in our own lives, we can read the Bible to find out how he acted with the ancient Hebrews, through Jesus, and in the early Christian community. If we want to know our own responsibilities in this interaction, we look in the Bible. If we need insight for decisions, the Scripture will offer good advice.

To be sure, the written word of God is not a simple book. But in the very process of trying to understand it, something happens within us. We stretch. We grow emotionally, intellectually, spiritually. We *become* more by encountering the word in writing. The Word of God *is* alive and active. It gives insight, correction, information. Most important of all, it can be the means to the lovely meeting with the Lord that our heart seeks.

Does this mean that the Word of God is a collection of literal facts about everything? Hardly! Because God spoke to the ancient Hebrews and early Christians in ways they would understand firsthand, some cultural translation is helpful (sometimes even necessary) for us. That means work, but the working is itself a meeting with God. It is not that we study and work and then God comes; God is present in the process of our searching for meanings in his written word. We need only to recognize him there.

For me, this is why Scripture is called the Word of God; not primarily because it gives us information. I'd like to have quite a bit of information that is not in the Bible. But the process of searching the Bible to meet God is sacred—and it works. God does come to meet those who search for him through the Bible.

The Sunday Mass offers us a way of focusing our ongoing encounter with God: three readings a week plus one psalm. We can take them as divine guidance toward the growth God offers us; we can take them as instruction for practice toward new, more loving, more fulfilling habits in our living and our praying. The readings can sustain us in difficulty and steady our lives more and more in the love of God.

Scripture is, in fact, just as nourishing to our spirit as is Eucharist; both are the Word of God in different form. The Bible is the written Word of God; the Eucharist is the Word made flesh, the body of the Lord.

Understanding the Readings

Of course, it is hard to be nourished by something we do not understand. Scripture is not like an intravenous feeding, dripping automatically into our souls. It is like good, hearty bread that must be bitten and chewed and digested in our consciousness. It is an active process. We begin it by giving ourselves basic understanding about the Scripture—and not only the gospels.

Today many resources are available to provide an overview of the Bible and its basic ideas and history. We Catholics can no longer maintain that we don't have Catholic materials on the Bible. Two good beginning books, in paperback, are *Reading the Old Testament* by Lawrence Boadt and *Reading the New Testament* by Pheme Perkins. If you read through only these two, your understanding of the readings at Mass will be immensely enhanced—to say nothing of how much more interesting they will become.

If you find that you want more Scripture study, ask your diocesan adult education office about the location of study groups. Request one in your own parish, or better yet, start one yourself. If you study alone, it is wise to ask the advice of someone who knows the field of Scripture better than you do, because not everything in print about the Bible will promote your growth.

An easy way to help yourself understand the Sunday Mass readings is to follow this simple procedure.

First, recall that the readings have been chosen according to a pattern so that the bulk of the Bible is read to us over three years (if we go to daily Mass). The reading from the Old Testament is chosen to complement and enrich the gospel. The psalm gives us a wonderful prayer about the same theme. The second reading usually offers an alternate theme, but it may provide another aspect of meaning for the other selections.

Preparing for the Readings

Before you go to Mass, look up the readings in your Bible. Then check a Bible commentary such as *The New Jerome*

Biblical Commentary or a Bible dictionary such as *Harper's Bible Dictionary*. These reference books are indispensable to anyone who wants the Word of God to be truly useful. They will reward your investment for many years.

When you have read these helps on the day's readings, write in a special notebook what strikes you as most important, what message you get for yourself, and any questions you have. Think a little about how you might apply these ideas in your own life during the coming week.

Then pray to God for more understanding of what God wants you to get from these readings at this time. Reread them prayerfully, expecting God to draw your heart to what is most important for you. Don't try to figure out exactly what the biblical writer was saying to the whole world. Try to get a glimpse of what God is saying to you personally, right now. The Spirit will help you—you can count on it.

This weekly routine can be done in half an hour or so, the time it takes to watch a sitcom or game show. Which is more important to you? Go to God if you have an issue with time; ask him to show you how to make time for his Word.

The results of personal weekly preparation of the Scripture readings for Mass cannot be calculated. It can deepen your relationship with the Lord immediately. It can guide you in decisions and help you in every area of need, from the least to the most critical. It can transform the quality of your life. It will definitely vitalize your prayer.

If you can share your scriptural preparation with your spouse, your children, or your friends, so much the better. You will grow even faster then, in ways you cannot now suspect. It can be a thrilling adventure!

Then you take your own discoveries to Mass in your heart and mind. When the Old Testament is read, you will already know the context of the reading and it will not seem so foreign and disconnected from your life. And if the reading jumps into the middle of a story (as they sometimes do), you will know how it began. When the New Testament is read, the words will speak directly to you.

You will listen differently, too. You already know a little. Now you want to hear the readings afresh. You are more alert. You listen for new understandings, perhaps the very insights you have already prayed for.

You will also listen differently to the homily. You will want your questions answered in the homilist's reflections. His insights will complement your own. You will find yourself in silent dialogue with the readings and the homily. Your appreciation of them will grow. No longer will you be listening in a half-blank fog!

The Homily

You and I know that many priests are wonderful homilists; they pray and prepare personally and diligently for each homily. We also know that some priests are more gifted in other areas. Only the Apostle Paul thought he had to be all things to all people, as he said in 1 Corinthians 9:22.

If we prepare the readings as part of our own spiritual growth—as we will, if we hunger for God's word active in our lives—then the good homilist will strengthen us, and the poor homilist will not leave us without food, because we will have prepared our own meal.

It is no accident that the first half of the Mass is called the Liturgy of the Word and the second half the Liturgy of the Eucharist. They belong together in our interior life. Either is incomplete without the other. They are the two halves of the foundation of our spiritual home. They are two vital means of experiencing God in our hearts and knowing ourselves in God's heart. Let us engage ourselves actively in both so we can be fully opened to God's gift of himself.

CHAPTER FIVE

Our Profession of Faith

At every Sunday Mass, we recite our Profession of Faith, either from memory or by reading it. It is so familiar that it has become nearly automatic. Is it too much to wonder if we actually know what we are saying?

The Profession of Faith, or Creed, is an amazing and wonderful document. It originated long ago, at the First Ecumenical (meaning universal) Council, held in 325 at Nicaea, a small town in present-day Turkey. Like all the early councils, the Nicene Council was called to define Christian belief amid proliferating opinions. Councils usually issued statements about "true" Christian belief as distinguished from other opinions, which were then called heresies.

The earlier councils were not universal, having been held in secret during the two and a half centuries that Christianity was illegal. In 311 Christianity was legalized, and in 325 the first public council was held. Part of the Nicene Creed was formulated there and another part at another Council in 381. Smaller portions were formed much later as needed. The last addition was made by the Emperor Charlemagne, who reigned from 800 to 814, causing a rift between Eastern and Western

Christianity that is still not healed today. The formulation we repeat at each Mass embodies about five hundred years of reflection, but its core is nearly sixteen hundred years old.

Christian Experience and the Spiritual Life

In spite of the passionate politicking in the early councils, two criteria for final decisions carried great weight. One was "Is this understanding true to Christian *experience*?" The other was "What would this formulation imply for Christian spiritual life, for one's innermost relationship with Christ?"

When I began to study early Christian history, it was a revelation to learn that the earliest leaders thought that experience and spiritual life were of central importance. It surprised me because today we are heirs to a great many doctrinal *words*. We learn the "correct" words and thoughts often before we have any experience of God or Christ to connect them to. Getting the formulas right has too often been our first training in Christianity.

In the earliest centuries there were no "right" words. There was only the invitation to *experience* Jesus Christ and to build one's life around him. From that experience, people tried to express what life and God meant to them, how they understood what they found within their own hearts. Any experience of Christ is essentially beyond expression in words; words are only pointers to the experience they try to express. The more profound and wonderful our Christian experience is, the less adequate are the words we use to share it with others.

So it is with the Creed. It cannot possibly express the glorious experience of God in Christ that early Christians knew and that can still be ours. The council participants tried to ensure that their formulations would support rather than violate profound Christian spiritual experience. Even then, it was a complicated task, requiring intense effort.

Knowing this, is it possible to use the Creed, that ancient collection of words and concepts, to bring us to our own deeper experience of Christ?

Words and Symbols of the Creed

Our understanding of symbol can help. You will recall that a true symbol is something that by its nature participates in more than one level of being and that it can draw us to higher levels of experience if we allow it. In this sense, the Creed is a symbol. (Remember, that does *not* mean it stands for something else; every true symbol is real in its own right.)

The Creed touches first our reason. All words are symbols, communicating concepts. The words of the Creed give us concepts consistent with early Christian experience. The concepts offer something fuller, they invite us to our own inner spiritual experience in Christ. Because they give us truth at the level of reason, they also imply the possibility of experiencing God's truth in our heart—the truth that the Creed has tried to express in symbol, in words.

How can we cooperate with this intention behind the Creed, this wonderful possibility of experiencing its truth? First, we begin where we are. We apply our mental understanding to the words of the Creed, paying attention to what we are saying every week. We want to understand what we profess to believe.

This is well within your power. Just read the Creed carefully and thoughtfully. If you wish to delve further into the meaning of the words, find a book on the Creed and explore the theology behind each phrase. That can be a monumental study—but what riches you will discover!

In the limited space we have here, we can only take a quick look at the meanings behind the words of the Creed.

The first paragraph is about God the Father. It asserts that God is a parent, that God is all-powerful, and that God has created and continues to create everything that exists in all realms of being, visible and invisible. God is a loving parent, powerful enough to make and control the whole universe—the totally benevolent power in all. Isn't this a wonderful foundation for our individual living? It is the basis of everything good, isn't it?

The second paragraph is about the Son of God. The strong affirmation here is that *there is no difference* between the Son and God; they are one in essence. The Creed stresses "begotten, not made." A created thing is differentiated from the creator; a "begotten" thing is *essentially* of the same nature as the begetter. So it is with the Son of God, "one in being with the Father."

The significance of that oneness for us is described next: the eternal Son took on human nature, became a human being, Jesus. At this part of the Creed, we are directed to bow. Few do it. Why is it recommended? This is the point of importance for every Christian. This is the Incarnation. God the Son became human *for our sake*, for the sake of our highest spiritual possibility, union with God the Trinity. We are asked to bow in reverence for that stupendous act of God and in thankful acceptance of the gift of the Incarnation.

According to the earliest Christian theologians, the Incarnation happened that we might be one with Christ in God; that we might be, by God's grace, what Christ is by nature, a child of the Father in full union with God. That was and is the point of all Christianity.

The third part of the Creed traces the events of Jesus' historical life that relate most closely to our spiritual potential: birth (he was truly human), passion, death, burial (his death was real), resurrection. Then follows Jesus' ascension and return to his eternal position as God. Birth, death, resurrection, ascension: the vital events that open infinite doors of spiritual development to us. *How* this works has been the subject of centuries of theology; *that* it works is the testimony of countless Christian saints. In the Creed, we simply assert that these events are the basis of our hope for oneness with God, as Jesus experienced, as many Christians have experienced.

Then the future coming of Christ is asserted, along with the expectation that time will be no more and Christ will be everything.

The fourth part of the Creed speaks of the Holy Spirit and again mentions theological formulations. Important for us is that the Spirit *gives life* to us, the life of the heart that beats for God. Also important is that the Spirit inspires all prophets, those who speak the truth of their experience in God to the people of their time. We listen to them because the Spirit is the divine force behind their words.

The fifth part of the Creed brings us to our present; each clause is clear if you look closely at it.

Your Personal Creed-Prayer

Now review the Creed, and ask yourself this question: *What would my life be like if any of these main ideas were not true?* Ponder this with your mind and your heart. What if God were not? What if the Incarnation had not happened? What if the Spirit were not? Don't ask about worldwide implications. Ask just about your own personal situation without these truths.

Next, ask yourself if you really accept, intellectually, what you say every week in the Creed. If you are not so sure about some of it, let your uncertainty take you on an inner search—

and maybe an outer one—to discover exactly what your questions are and how Christian tradition has answered them. You could hardly have objections that no one *ever* thought of before!

As you work with the ideas, ask yourself over and over, *What does this mean to me?* Feed your mind with theology if you like, but decide for yourself what you mean when you say the Creed—and if you can truthfully say it all. If you can't, then don't. Honesty before the Lord is essential to spiritual growth and maintains your integrity in worship.

Next, measure your own spiritual experience against the Creed. Ask yourself these questions: *Have I really known God the Father in my heart? Have I experienced Jesus the Son in reality or just in history? Does the Spirit inspire me? Do I want spiritual experience? What is my experience of forgiveness? Do I expect resurrection?*

Notice where you feel gaps or shallows in your experience. Where could it be filled out? Take your insights to prayer. Lay them before the Lord and ask him how to cooperate with his deepening of your relationship with him. The Spirit will tell you—that's the Spirit's job, too!

When you have worked with the Creed for a while, you will begin to notice that some things follow naturally on well-considered belief. First, what we truly believe, we act upon. It becomes the basis for decisions, choices, and events in our daily life. Second, if we really believe the Creed, giving ourselves to the Father, Son, and Spirit is only logical. If we "get it," how could we refuse ourselves to such astounding love, such powerful action on our behalf? We will move naturally and heartily beyond merely conventional religion.

Notice that if our living is grounded in the realities expressed in the Creed, we have a solid place in life. We are recipients of the greatest divine gift, God himself, and we respond to that gift. When we know that, gradually everything in our life takes its proper perspective. Everything else can be based on that recognition. Try it out next time you must make a decision. Think *Who am I? I am a receiver of God's gifts, and I respond in kind.* Then choose and act.

Finally, you can make the Creed a personal prayer about your relationship to Father, Son, Spirit, and the Church. Instead of saying it *about* God, say it *to* God: "We believe in you. You are one God. You are the Father. You are the Almighty." "We believe in you. You are one Lord, Jesus Christ. You are the only Son of God. You are eternally begotten." "We believe in you, Holy Spirit. You are the Lord. You are the giver of life."

Why do I not suggest that you make the "we" into an "I"? Because by saying this Creed-prayer you identify with the Christian community of all the centuries, from the very first disciples until today. Jesus prayed in John 17 that all his followers be one with the Father *and* with one another. When we focus on this central expression of Christian belief, it is not the time to separate ourselves from other Christians. So as you pray the Creed, be fully aware of your participation in the communal faith and—God willing—the spiritual experience of all Christians.

Perhaps you will find that a thoughtful, honest, and grateful Creed-prayer begins to open your heart to receive the experience of the early Christians, which they valued so much that they wanted to safeguard it through these ancient words. If it does open your heart, the Creed as symbol will have done its work and *you* will be closer to union with the Lord.

CHAPTER SIX

We Intercede for Others

The Mass is a source of spiritual power for the Christian. Moreover, its parts form a pattern for our spiritual exercises, that is, what we actually do in our spiritual life.

The first major section of the Mass, the Liturgy of the Word, closes with our general intercessions. Recall what has happened up to this point. We have cleared our relationship with God by penitence and praise. We have heard God's Word through Scripture and preaching, reminding us of our Christian purpose and how to fulfill it. And we have announced our basic convictions in Christian faith—the Creed.

By this point in the Mass, then, our inner state is improved. We are more open, more ready, more steady, more aware of our foundation in Christ. All our heart and our attention is connected once again with the roots of our Christianity. It is a little like getting one's feet firmly planted before sprinting the one-hundred-yard dash. It's necessary for a solid and rapid takeoff. So now at Mass, we are solidly set. From that inner position, we pray best for others.

Our Priestly Function

Intercession is a vital function in Christian life. First of all, it's a pretty egocentric person who does not pray for others. Active Christians pray for those they love.

Moreover, intercession is a particular call to every Christian because, as the *St. Joseph Missal* says, "All Christians share in Christ's royal priesthood, which is a function of intercession for all." A priest is one who stands, as it were, between God and another person to plead on that person's behalf. Christ is our high priest; and, of course, our ordained priests do the same thing. What we often ignore is that every Christian bears that same priestly duty in relation to other people and to all the world. At the general intercessions, we exercise our priestly function as a community. We are called do the same as individuals.

Jesus prayed for others. The most familiar example is in John 17, when Jesus prayed for his disciples just before he was crucified. Paul tells us that Christ still intercedes for us. (See Romans 8:34.) The Letter to the Hebrews states it even more strongly: Christ "has a priesthood that does not pass away. Therefore, he is always able to save those who approach God through him, since he lives forever to make intercession for them" (Hebrews 7:24-25).

Early Christians prayed for one another. Paul wrote repeatedly of his prayer for the young Christian communities and begged their prayers for him. A few examples you may look up include Philippians 1:9-11, Romans 15:30-32, Colossians 1:3, and 2 Corinthians 1:11.

In the First Letter to Timothy, Paul urges that intercession be a regular part of individual and community life: "I ask that supplications, prayers, petitions, and thanksgivings be offered for everyone, for kings and for all in authority....This is good and pleasing to God" (2:1-3). The intercessions at Mass still fulfill Paul's request today.

All One Body

What are we really doing when we pray for others, individually or at liturgy? Are we informing God and telling him to pay attention and get moving? That sounds silly—and it is. Intercession is important, but not because it can tell God anything he doesn't already know.

The power of intercession is rooted in the reality that God does not force gracious gifts on people. We have to be in condition to receive divine blessings. Praying for others helps us acquire the inner conditions required.

At the root of our being, we are all one Body of Christ. If we could see to the very deepest center of ourselves, we would find the reality that we are never totally separated from one another. The mystical saints insist from experience that we are truly all one, that everything we do affects everyone else. If we usually think of the Body of Christ as including only Christians, we can remind ourselves that Jesus died for all people. So there is a "one-body-ness," so to speak, embracing all of humanity.

Most of us experience our human unity as deep concern for others, those we know and those we don't know. Charitable organizations are kept alive by people who care about people they don't know personally. Disasters are alleviated out of the same human love. We bring food to church for the poor, whether we know the recipients or not.

When we pray for others, we actually do uplift the whole body of humanity. We act as a sort of connector, like a lamp plug. We plug ourselves into the main current for the purpose of turning on the light so the light can shine for all. We connect ourselves to God so God can act through our prayer to give to all. When we pray for others, each of us is one member of the Body of Christ taking care of other members of the Body.

A Generous Offering of Self

At Mass, intercessions may seem so easy that we say the right words but hardly notice what we are praying for. Intercession as a true priestly function is not easy, however. Real intercession, at Mass or at home, requires self-offering. We give our love and concern to God and to others. We make ourselves available as conduits for the love of God to reach others. People who pray intensely for others find it a real sacrifice of themselves—their energy, their attention, their compassion, their time. If prayer for others is real, it will cost something.

Genuine heartfelt intercession requires a generous heart—a heart with compassion in its center. The more attention we give to other people, the stronger our inner compassion becomes. The more intense our compassion, the more powerful our prayer for others. The converse is also true: the more we practice our Christianity by praying for others, the more compassion will flow warmly from our heart.

In fact, it is doubtful if intercession is effective unless we pray with loving self-offering. Automatic responses (or other kinds of indifference) have little effect on anyone or anything. The intercessions at Mass, with our responses, can change a life, alter circumstances, heal and warm and comfort—if they cost us love.

If we are faithful to the two greatest commandments, we will love both God and people. When you have two friends you love dearly, isn't it a treat if you bring them together and they enjoy each other? So also, when we love both God and others, we naturally talk to God about our loved ones. For those we do not easily love, but are commanded to love, we can pray for goodness in their lives—and we will begin to love them, just as Christ does.

Effective Intercession

Chances are, if we do not pray for others regularly and wholeheartedly, the intercessions at Mass won't mean much to us. Here again, we see that our participation in the Mass and our personal spiritual efforts affect one another. If we want our Mass to be as alive as it can be, we will practice intercessory prayer on our own as well. How can we do it effectively?

First, we can do it regularly. If we already have a regular time for prayer, we can include our intercessory prayer then. Some people keep a list of names or a packet of photographs of people for whom they are praying. Some write their names in a journal. Whatever memory aid you choose, praying regularly for others will both help them and enlarge your own loving heart.

Second, before we begin, we may check our attitudes. If we are praying for others when we are full of fears, we had best not do it, for we will only be pouring fear into the situation. That is never helpful. To pray well for others, we may have to struggle with ourselves until we can pray purely from an attitude of love. In times of crisis, that is a huge challenge unless we have been doing it all along. So let's start now to examine our own feelings before we send them out to God for others.

Then we want to pray open-ended prayers. We can freely ask for what we think is good and right, but we must be willing to let go of our opinions and turn everything over to God for decision and action. Very often, God is ready to give something better than we can imagine. Since God loves us as well as those for whom we are praying, we can trust him. The most profound secret of effective prayer for others is relinquishment: turning loose the whole issue, the whole person, to God.

If we find relinquishment difficult, we may want to check our motivations. Are we praying for another because we ourselves want a certain thing to happen? If so, then isn't our prayer actually more selfish than intercessory? And second, do we really trust that God knows *better* than we do what is truly good for the other person? If not, perhaps we need to pray for an increase of trust.

The Simple Movement of a Christian Heart

To avoid stumbling over selfishness or lack of trust, here is a particular way to pray beautifully and powerfully for others. Quiet yourself as profoundly as you can. If you already practice a form of centering prayer or contemplative prayer, do that. Then, when you are centered, gently and simply bring to God a bare thought of the person or situation for which you want to pray. Say nothing about it to God—no explanation, no request, no begging. Simply hold your attention gently on God's love and simultaneously on the person you're praying for. Keep them together until you yourself feel a sense of completion or an awareness of peace. Then let it go and return to your contemplative practice. You can be sure that such simple prayer of love has been heard and is changing something.

When I was a teenager, I heard a woman speak whose ministry was healing. She told of taking a very sick baby in her arms and simply holding him while loving God and opening to God's love for the infant. The baby was well in a few hours.

I thought then—and still think—that hers is a most glorious vocation. Then she went on to say that the Lord had guided her to know that in order for healing to occur through her, she must practice praying three hours every day. And she had!

Powerful intercession is not for lukewarm Christians. But the simple movement of a Christian heart in compassion for others is also intercession—and to that we are all called, individually and at every Mass.

So the next time you participate in the Mass, remember that intercession is a vital part of it. If you already pray individually for others, your participation in the Liturgy of the Word will prepare you for sincere and loving intercession. Then you will pray for others with a clear heart—a heart that God can use to change things, if it is his loving will.

CHAPTER SEVEN

We Have These Gifts to Offer

A man gave a particularly lovely necklace to his wife. She was thrilled. A few weeks later, the husband saw her necklace adorning the sweater of another woman, one known to have severe financial struggles. When he asked his wife about it, she said she had given the necklace to this woman, because "she has so little beauty in her life." The husband was insulted and angry.

We can all understand his feelings, can't we? And yet we must ask, Why did the husband give the gift? Was it a truly free gift for her to do with as she wished? Or was it for the pleasure *he* got out of seeing the necklace on his wife?

What is the meaning of a gift? What is the meaning of the offering at the Mass?

What the Gifts Symbolize

At Mass, the gifts are bread, wine, and money. It can only be said that "we" offer them, *if* each of us does join our *self* to these gifts to offer all to God.

What do these gifts symbolize? Bread and wine recall the

last supper Jesus shared with his disciples. They ate bread and drank wine because it was everyday fare. The gifts are food, nourishment necessary for living. So our bread and wine at Mass represent our everyday lives, our everyday selves, the essence of our lives.

We also offer money. What does money mean to us? In our society, money is closely involved with our sense of selfhood, our sense of privacy (how many people know how much money you make?), our sense of worth and status. It affects almost everything, certainly our possessions and experiences. When people list what they want in life, money almost always ranks high. The point is not to argue with society's values, but simply to note them. Money does mean a lot to us. That is exactly the spiritual reason for offering money to God—because it bears so much of our personal identity.

The real gift at the offertory of the Mass is the gift of ourselves. The physical items we offer symbolize, at their deepest level, our own being. Whether the gifts are proffered in silence or in song, the ritual will have meaning for us only insofar as we are offering our own selves (or our day or our week) along with the gifts.

The Gift of Ourselves

In self-offering, we emulate the Holy Trinity. One way of thinking about the interior relationship of the three Persons is that each continually offers himself to the others: Father to Son, Son to Father, each to Spirit and Spirit to each. There is eternal self-offering in the heart of God. To be true to this constant giving, we give ourselves to God, who offers himself also to us interiorly.

Why do we offer anything? Our motives will match the level of our spiritual maturity. We may give in order to receive gifts from God. While such exchange does indeed occur, if it is our chief motivation, we still have some growing to do. Giving *in order* to receive is a form of business with God—good business no doubt, but hardly an offering of oneself.

If we offer ourselves out of gratitude and love for God, leaving ourselves open to the Lord, we are closer to a true relationship with the Lord. Can you imagine the Persons of the Trinity withholding themselves from one another? Likewise, have not all of them given themselves wholly *for* us in the Son?

In total self-offering, at Mass and everywhere, there is only love and great joy. It is built into our nature to give out of love and to experience great joy in the giving. We are, at the center, the image of God, the true "offerer" and the true offering.

Preparation of the Gifts

The preparation of the gifts, now at the altar, reflects the beautiful in our giving to God. We bless the Lord for divine goodness. We acknowledge that only because of God's generosity do we even have gifts to offer. Here we do not give because we are "supposed to." Here we give from hearts full of gratitude for the goodness we have received. If that is not the case, we should keep silent.

We also acknowledge that in our giving we are equally dependent on the earth itself and on other people's efforts. We give in awareness of our true condition, interdependence with our environment and with all human beings. The bread and wine are not usually made by our own hands, but they are made by human hands, and their elements come from the earth.

The same is true of our money, except that we have the choice to withhold it from offering. None of us is self-sufficient. We may have earned our money, but behind our ability to earn is an institution with its people, the folks who schooled us or trained us, the people who receive our product or other results of our work. It is like one big net, and each of us is a knot in that net. All of us depend on the net of the whole for our very life.

In that awareness, we offer our money to God. Perhaps a good question to ask ourselves is this: Do we try to determine what God will do with our gift of dollars?

As the priest prepares the gifts to be sacrificed to God, he prays the vital prayer that expresses what the Mass—and the Christian life—is intended to be for us. It may not be spoken aloud, but it is there. As he drops a little ordinary water into the wine he prays: "By the mystery of this water and wine, may we come to share in the divinity of Christ, who humbled himself to share in our humanity."

A Stupendous Hope

The symbolism here enhances the gesture for us. Wine, though everyday fare, has always symbolized divinity as well. A discussion of all the symbolic connections of wine would be too long to include here. Briefly, though, it is more than water, it affects us, it has the color of blood (life), it is liquid and fiery simultaneously. Consider the "mystique" that every culture builds around the making and drinking of wine. It has a quality beyond ordinary drinking water.

In the preparation of the gifts, the water symbolizes our ordinary human nature and the wine symbolizes the divine nature. A little of the water mixes with the wine, gets lost in the wine, participates in the wine. Just so, the prayer says, "May we come to share in the divinity of Christ...."

This point has been made before, but it is so vital to spiritual life and to full participation in the Mass that we must reflect on it again. The earliest Christians experienced Christ in their lives. They participated in the Eucharist because it helped them keep their experience alive. The Eucharist *is* that experience if entered with a fully open heart. Christ gave his disciples the possibility of being children of God by grace, just as he was Son of God by nature. Jesus came to give himself to us, in us. That is no figure of speech; it is not an abstraction. It is the truth and it can be experienced.

To receive our Lord fully is precisely what the Mass offers to us, and it is what we pray for as the gifts are offered and prepared. It is also the hope and alm of our relationship with God, our spiritual life. It is God's loving hope for us.

Is it business with God to desire this union? The saints have said there is only one wholly good desire: to be one with the Lord. When we offer ourselves wholly in this loving desire, it is not business. There is this difference: in our heart, we leave God free to say "Wait" or even "No." We give ourselves wholly when we give simply for love, no matter what God will then do with us.

We understand this already. Indeed, our understanding sometimes prevents us from giving ourselves because we are afraid of what God might do with us! We may not yet know in our bones that everything God does is for love, for our joy, and for our truest good.

What can we do about offering? At Mass, we must be honest. We offer whatever we can in the warmest love we presently experience. If we can offer only the change in our pockets, with a tiny intention for "someday," then we do so honestly. If we can lay our whole selves on the altar in overflowing love for the Lord, we do that. Most of us are probably somewhere in-between. Give it some thought: what do *you* offer at Mass? What is your real motivation for it?

When the gifts are ready, we—the community—pray that they may be acceptable to God. What does that mean? It may be analogous to what we hope for when we give gifts to loved ones. We hope they will like them, use them, find them beautiful. But isn't it even more? We hope that they know by our gift that we love them. We hope that they love us, too, and will show it by accepting the gift we offer. We don't want them to love us *because* of the gift, but for ourselves. The accepted gift, then, symbolizes our mutual love. It is this we hope for from God: shared love and its joyousness.

We ask God to accept our gifts for "the praise and glory of his name, for our good, and the good of all his Church." We pray that the outcome of our giving will be God's glory and goodness in the earth. We know that this prayer is in accord with the divine Will.

When we offer ourselves, the bread, and the wine in the Mass, we call them a "sacrifice." Since many of us think sacrifice means killing something, or at least being in pain over it, we may miss its essential meaning. The word *sacrifice* comes from two Latin words which mean "to make sacred" or "to make holy." What happens in the sacrifice of the Mass is that our gifts are accepted by God at a spiritual level of reality and transformed into something sacred, holy. Of course, that transformation happens concretely to the bread and wine at each Mass. It can happen just as concretely to us, our very selves, over time, as we continue to offer ourselves more and more wholly to the Lord. We too can be made into Christ—that is what it's all about.

A Closing Suggestion

Before you go to Mass the next time, take a few minutes and quiet yourself. Ponder this question: *Just what is it that I offer at the offertory of the Mass?* Can you discover how much of yourself you really want God to control? Try to find words for it, just for yourself. Ask yourself if you are fully satisfied with your present level of self-offering. Then ask whether in your deepest heart you honestly *want* to "participate in the divinity of Christ" in this very life. Not everyone does, and it is important for the spiritual life to know what sort of goal you hold dear.

Honesty is crucial to this inquiry. When you have completed it, turn it into a prayer. Write it down and take it with you to Mass next time. Pray it silently in your heart during the offertory. Offer it just for love.

CHAPTER EIGHT

Our Eucharistic Prayers

The centerpiece of every Mass is the eucharistic prayer. At the heart of that prayer is the consecration, the moment in which our bread and wine become the body and blood of Jesus Christ, our Lord.

From all time, in every faith, whatever is most holy and most powerful has been surrounded by ritual and prayer. In our tradition, these rituals and prayers serve two functions. They are real prayer, consciously offered to God by his people the Church from our own hearts. They also communicate to us, again and again, the beauty and content of that most sacred moment of consecration.

In my early days as a Catholic (with a theological education behind me) when the Mass was still new, it struck me so forcefully that in the Eucharist we have a genuine source of power to enrich our lives and draw us ever closer to God. I have not always been able to keep the force of that insight, but I haven't forgotten its truth. At every Mass, we have the possibility of returning to the source of our faith, the source of our being, and to receive again the magnificent benefits God wishes to give us.

The opportunity by itself is not enough to make God's

gifts actual, however. If we go to Mass only as an obligation or a social habit, very little will happen in us or for us. If we sit dully in our pews daydreaming about yesterday's shopping trip or this afternoon's football game, that most holy moment, the consecration, will go by without our notice. A great pity.

We can, however, find ways to increase our capacity for interest and attention. One of those "how-tos" is to notice what is happening in the eucharistic prayer and to begin to incorporate its contents into our own ongoing spiritual growth.

On one hand, the eucharistic prayer may seem repetitive because we hear one of them at every Mass. (There are four major eucharistic prayers, as well as special prayers for particular times, such as children's Masses and Masses of reconciliation.) On the other hand, these prayers may seem too complicated to follow clearly. If we look closely at the structure and content of the eucharistic prayers, we will be able to follow and appreciate them more easily. We'll know what to listen for.

An Invitation to Praise

The eucharistic prayer is always introduced by an invitation to lift our hearts to the Lord and give him thanks. This we say in dialogue form with the priest.

Then comes the preface. The preface is not always the same, since special prefaces are available for special occasions. All prefaces, though, are prayers of honor and thanksgiving to God, ending with an invitation to praise God along with the heavenly hosts. Then, together we sing the praise-filled *Sanctus*: Holy, Holy, Holy!

Have you ever wondered where this song came from? The first part of it is a slightly altered quotation from Isaiah 6:3. The prophet experienced this holy Lord in a vision and heard the heavenly seraphim singing this song of praise to God. I recommend that you read Isaiah 6:1-8 for the whole story. It is one of the loveliest in the Old Testament.

The second part, Hosanna, is taken from Mark 11:9. It is the praise the crowd offered Jesus as he entered Jerusalem on a donkey's back.

The Structure of the Eucharistic Prayers

Although the eucharistic prayers are different in emphasis and each includes unique elements, their topics are the same. A comparison shows the following likenesses.

Each begins with praise to the Father, to whom the whole prayer is addressed. The length varies from two lines to most of a page. The longest one, the fourth, sounds almost like a sermon if not read prayerfully. It is actually a remembering, a reflection on the great events that have led to our faith and salvation. But it is addressed to God as the giver of all those blessings.

All except the first prayer invoke the Holy Spirit's blessing on the gifts; all the prayers request that the gifts become "the body and blood" of Jesus Christ.

Of course, all the eucharistic prayers review the Last Supper Jesus had with his disciples, during which the consecration occurs.

The priest invites us to "proclaim the mystery of faith," which we do by one of four possibilities (or more if the acclamation of faith is sung).

Reflecting Jesus' self-offering to the Father, the eucharistic prayer continues by briefly recalling the last events in Jesus' earthly life and by formally offering to the Father the sacrifice now made holy by the consecration. This part closes with a prayer for unity among us all in the Holy Spirit.

The remainder of the prayer has three sections, which appear in all eucharistic prayers but in differing order: a prayer for the Church, a prayer for unity with the saints, and a prayer for the dead.

All close with the same praise: "Through him, with him, in him, in the unity of the Holy Spirit, all glory and honor is yours, almighty Father, for ever and ever. Amen."

Now let's look at each of these topics to see how they might teach us more about our own life with God. We can use the content of the prayers for further guidance.

PRAISE THE FATHER BY REMEMBERING

We begin with praise and thanksgiving, the original meaning of *eucharist*. Praise takes many forms in our life and in the Bible. In the eucharistic prayers, it takes a form similar to a public tribute to a loved one, such as an honored teacher or benefactor. In public we recount to the honored one and to others all the beautiful and splendid contributions they have made, the generous gifts they have given, their good qualities, and their accomplishments. That is like the opening praise in the eucharistic prayers.

It is a lovely pattern for our own praise. Entering fully into the eucharistic prayer will help us learn how to do it ourselves if we don't already. In the context of the Mass, of course, we pray to God about those wonderful things he has done for all people. We trace the whole history of his relationship to the human race through creation, through Israel, through Jesus and the Holy Spirit, through the Church.

If we make this kind of prayer our own, we surely will be grateful for those great gifts. Yet we are often more aware of the things God has done individually for us and those we love. Do we go over those and tell God again and again how grateful we are for them? Do we remind him of his goodness to us, just the way we might speak to a loved spouse about her or his goodness? "Lord, you did this...and this...and this...for me, and I love you for it. I'm so grateful. It's done so much for me."

Does this kind of prayer seem too simple to you? Well, that's one of its beauties. It is simple. It is childlike—and Jesus warned us that we must become like children to enter his glorious kingdom.

Seek the Holy Spirit

In the eucharistic prayers, the Holy Spirit is invoked for a particular purpose: that our offerings of bread and wine be transformed and sanctified.

In our own living, we could be calling on the Holy Spirit for everything imaginable. A friend of mine, a nun, has greatly impressed and taught me about this. She spontaneously and freely speaks to the Spirit about everything, little and big, expected and dreamed of, serious and funny. When I tried to imitate her, I discovered that I wasn't on such familiar terms with the Holy Spirit! My friend is constantly aware of the Spirit's presence, like some great invisible friend—which, of course, is exactly what the Holy Spirit really is.

As I practiced referring everything to the Spirit, I discovered that such prayer is easier than almost any other kind—when I remembered. That's what made the big difference. My friend doesn't have to consciously remember to do it, and I still do. But I remember more often now, and the results are delightful—more peace, intensified inner support, less sense of separation from other people, and a much more intimate awareness of God's constant presence.

One unexpected result is that I giggle more (although mostly not aloud). Why? I think it's because when more and more of one's life is simply given over into hands of the Spirit, life isn't as heavy. Life gets lighter, and some things that used to seem serious turn out to be downright funny. The Holy Spirit apparently did not mean for us to be solemn, but lighthearted.

The shock that came with this practice was the recognition that I (no doubt all of us) cling to solemnity more than I realized. When one begins to experience the difference between solemn living and lighthearted Spirit-ual living, the ego-centered self prefers the solemn. It takes itself so seriously! But because the Holy Spirit takes us quite lightly, we learn to do the same if we allow it to happen.

It was no accident that Jesus said, "My yoke is easy, and my burden light" (Matthew 11:30). It is simply true. So invoke the Holy Spirit for everything and in all circumstances. You'll be glad you did.

Praying for the Church

Let's turn next to the prayers of the Church for the Church. The "parts" of the Church are enumerated: pope, bishop, clergy, and people. We pray that all of us may be stronger in love and in faith, in peace and in unity, all over the world.

No doubt we all experience mixed feelings about the Church at times. We hold high ideals for it, and few in it seem to live up to those ideals—nor do we ourselves, if we are honest. How do we respond to the conflicts in the Church? How do we respond when Church leaders get in trouble, personal or professional?

A wonderful priest, long retired but still profoundly dedicated to his vocation, was recently heard to say that "the Church is still encumbered with human beings." It made us all laugh—but gently, because in our laughter was recognition that we also sometimes "encumber" the Church.

It is easy to find fault with the Church and Church people. But the eucharistic prayers show us a better way. Pray for the Church that it may fulfill the will of the Lord completely. Pray for the hierarchy, the priesthood, and everyone. We *all* need it.

The Church, after all, has brought great gifts to us in its tradition, its guidance, its mystical life, and especially in its loyalty to the Eucharist itself. Where would our spiritual life be without these gifts? Would we know the Lord? Would we have a spiritual life?

If we have a beloved friend who sometimes does strange and troublesome things or who sometimes gets sick, will we abandon that friend? Most of us probably wouldn't. If we couldn't change much, we would surely pray hard for our friend. Can we do less for the Church?

There is an additional step, though it is not mentioned in the eucharistic prayers. The Church as a whole will never be better than its members. We cannot change all of its members, perhaps not even a few, but we can do a lot for the Church by being, ourselves, as fully Christian as we possibly can be. So when we pray for the Church, let's explicitly include ourselves, that we, too, may be strengthened in love and faith, peace and unity, with all. Prayer for all of us together is an excellent practice for each of us, at any time.

Praying to Share With the Saints

All except the first eucharistic prayer simply pray that we may join with the saints in heaven. They express a desire to be with Mary, the Mother of God, then with the apostles, martyrs, and other saints.

The first prayer includes a longer section honoring the saints—Mary, Joseph, the apostles, and others. Some of them are named. It is a pity that many of these saints are virtually unknown to us in the pews, not that we couldn't find out about them if we wanted to. Resources are available. Some of the saints mentioned were early apostles named in the Bible. Others lived in the first several centuries of the Church, among them early popes and missionaries. Along with honoring them, we pray that their prayers will help us join them. The fourth prayer looks forward to joining the saints in God's heavenly "kingdom," where singing the glory of God will be our great occupation.

Why should we want to be joined with the saints? Do we know who they were, what they did, why they were canonized? Do we ponder their lives? Do we read about them? Do we talk about them with one another? Do we honor them individually and personally at other times than at Mass? Do we already have a concrete relationship with them? If we do all this, then we are already actively moving toward a deeper union with them.

The truth is, anyone who is joined sincerely to Jesus Christ is already joined in his mystical body with all other Christians, those alive on this earth and those alive in that mysterious state we call the "afterlife." The union of all Christians is real and more interior than exterior. And part of our union with the saints is surely a wish to be more and more like them.

Moreover, if we are committed to a growing closeness to Christ, we can count on the support of saints who sought and experienced union with the Lord. Those who have gone far in prayer never feel they have gone alone. Saints always accompany them, and their presence and help can be experienced.

Certainly, it is delusion to think we are alone in our spiritual efforts. If the Church is anything, it is a community of people who want to be close to God. Some of them are on Earth and some are not, but we all continue into God as long and as far as we want to. Saint Gregory of Nyssa said that growth into God is forever and unending, because God is infinite. So we pray to the saints, who may have gone much farther in the spiritual journey than we have, and ask for whatever help they can give.

The third eucharistic prayer says that we "rely for help" on the prayers of the saints. Do we do that consciously? It is a wonderful idea, this reliance by those who are still struggling—you and me—on the help of those who have attained. Give it some thought; then start to do it, or do it more often.

Praying for the Dead

At every Mass, we pray together for those who have left this life ahead of us. These prayers are based on the same conviction as our prayers to the saints: that we are all one in Christ, no matter at what level of development we may be. If we all belong to one another in love, we pray for one another with joy.

Many modern hearts feel a contradiction. On one hand, we'd like to think that our loved ones died straight into God's fullest presence. If so, why would we be praying for them? On the other hand, the Church continues to pray for those who have died recently and not so recently.

The Church has never said that a person dies automatically into the fullness of God. At various times, stages of life after physical death have been explained in different ways. Purgatory, probably the most familiar, is understood to be a state of purification continuing until the person is able to receive God in divine fullness. During this purification and continuing growth, we can help with our prayer for him or her. Don't let your questions about purgatory get too technical or too detailed. The truth is, nobody actually knows the answers to those specific questions about the afterlife.

For our life of prayer, we don't need specific answers—although, admittedly, the unknown is not usually comfortable for us. We need to cultivate a loving heart toward all who have died and to develop the practice of praying for them. It helps keep us close to those we know and love. It heightens our awareness of the Body of Christ, here as well as "there." Furthermore, isn't it wonderful to think that just as we have prayed for others, when we step into that vast unknown, others will be praying as a continuation of their love and support for us?

The Heart of the Eucharistic Prayers

There is surely no need to explain the prayer of consecration. As it is said, the great gift of Jesus to all his followers unfolds at every consecration, and he becomes fully and tangibly present in the sacrament of the altar. This is the center of the Church's life. It is the center of the individual Christian's life *insofar* as it is accepted and assimilated into one's mind and heart, one's whole being. It is thus like the other great gifts of God, faithfully and constantly given. The quality of benefits we receive depends on whether we are strong enough, willing enough, open enough, to assimilate them.

In a sense, the spiritual life is a continual opening to receive God in Christ. We open our hearts and our lives as much as we are able today, then more tomorrow, and more and more until we can be wholly God's, filled with the life of Christ. If in our hearts we pray the prayer of consecration, aware that we long to become filled with Christ and transformed into "other Christs," then our lives will increasingly open until the consecration becomes real in us.

The consecration prayer also reminds us that the liturgy

is a memorial of Jesus. We do it in memory of the Lord, especially of his human life and death. Remembering is a powerful practice in spiritual life. First of all, remembering God is necessary to the spiritual life. We humans *are* awfully forgetful! Yet if we are inwardly oblivious to God's presence, we can hardly live close to his heart. The more we long for God, the more we will remember God.

If our continuing forgetfulness distresses us, we can add practice in remembering to our other spiritual efforts. We can set aside a few minutes of our prayer time to recall what we know about Jesus, just in ourselves. We might use this time to study Scripture to learn more about God. Of course, going to daily Mass, where remembering is so pervasive, would be ideal. We might take up a short prayer, like the Jesus Prayer, to repeat whenever our mind slips into neutral. Silently repeating the name of Jesus or God will also help us remember. Then, our specific remembering of the Last Supper, passion and resurrection of our Lord at Mass will be rich with the content of our daily remembering, and our daily remembering will be revitalized in turn by attentive participation in the prayers around the consecration.

Our mental recalling of Christ's life and death will also remind us that the Eucharist is a sacramental memorial. The Eucharist makes present, in the spiritual/sacramental realm, not only the body and blood of Christ but also Jesus' atoning sacrifice—while, of course, in no way repeating it since it is unique, all sufficient, and unrepeatable.

One of the most striking notes in the comparison of the eucharistic prayers is that the first three mention Jesus' betrayal, suffering, and death. The fourth speaks only of Jesus' glorification—exactly as does the fourth gospel, the Gospel of John. Especially in John, the passion and the glorification were just two views of one single act in which Jesus was shown to be the Redeemer, the Son of God, the Lord we love.

The other striking thing about the consecration prayers is their double mention of praise and thanksgiving. Even facing directly into death and total personal sacrifice, Jesus' attitude was full of praise to the Father. It is a teaching.

If our hearts were filled with praise for our life, when suffering comes, how much room in our hearts can there be for pain? If our hearts are filled every day with thanksgiving, how much room can there be for resentments and fears? Our whole spiritual life and all the healing we need could occur so much more quickly and easily if we constantly praised God, constantly gave ourselves in thanks-filled offering, just as Jesus did at the Last Supper.

After the consecration, we are again reminded that this is a celebration of the memory of Jesus Christ and all he did and does for us. The first eucharistic prayer says, "We *celebrate* the memory of Christ." Celebration does not have to be slaphappy, but it is hardly true celebration when it is somber or boring. Both somberness and boredom come from within our own contracted hearts. They are not the result of anything exterior, although we generally do not take responsibility for them ourselves. Nevertheless, the memory of Jesus can be a joy, was meant to be a joy. In joy, our hearts celebrate life—ours as well as his. In joy we offer our sacred gifts.

Have you ever noticed how hard it is to give anything sincerely when you are full of resentment, self-pity, or some other negative emotion? It's almost impossible! Yet here, in the prayer of memory, we ask God to receive our offerings. We can only do that in truth if we are open at heart and if joy is dwelling there.

If the celebration of Christ's memory is not joyful for you, then you may wish to examine yourself and see why it is not. You can begin by looking at your relationship with Christ. If it is a shallow, nodding acquaintance, celebration is hardly relevant. If your relationship with him is intimate and true however, it is an adventure. Then celebration is as natural as breathing. Using your capacity for celebration of Jesus' memory as a measure, check the intensity of your relationship with the Lord. Then take what you learn about this relationship to prayer, where something can be done with them.

Let Us Attend!

In one of the earliest Masses, written by Saint John Chrysostom, whenever anything especially important is about to be read or said, the congregation is reminded: *Let us attend!* It is a needed reminder that has appeared before in these pages. It is especially vital at the time of consecration and communion. If we are not paying attention, we will not experience much renewal. And we so need renewal, over and over. It's a shame to let such empowerment go by. So, to the eucharistic prayers at the next Mass, *let us attend!*

CHAPTER NINE

After the eucharistic prayers, comes the communion rite itself. It both climaxes and completes our Mass. Before receiving communion, however, we pray in the form that Jesus taught his disciples.

THE LORD'S PRAYER

The Lord's Prayer is recorded in the gospels. One version is found in Matthew 6:9-13 as part of Jesus' teaching in the Sermon on the Mount. The other version is in Luke 11:2-4, where it is Jesus' response to the request of his disciples to "teach us to pray."

We customarily use the Lord's Prayer as a formula-prayer, one that we memorized as a child and repeat throughout our lives. As spiritual writer Anthony Bloom pointed out, however, being quoted does not mean being used. The question for our deeper spiritual life is, how can we *use* this prayer of Jesus?

If we repeat the Lord's Prayer only mechanically, it is unlikely to affect our relationship with the Lord. Too easily it becomes just automatic words—the brain works and maybe the mouth, but the heart is not involved. Yet to commune with the Lord, our heart must be wholly involved. The Lord's Prayer, if we use it deliberately and attentively, can bring the whole of ourselves to God.

A Pattern for Interior Prayer

Scripture scholars and theologians often agree that Jesus may not have meant this prayer to be primarily a formula-prayer for repetition. Many think it was intended to be a *pattern* for our interior prayer. Every phrase is rich with possible meaning and association; every phrase can be used as source for extended meditation. Every phrase relates to our inner life with God.

We will begin with a few hints of possible meanings. If you follow up with experiment and reflection of your own, the Lord's Prayer will open more of its treasures to you.

God, Our Loving Parent

Let us start with the center of everything: *Our Father*. Those words expressed Jesus' intense and intimate relationship with God. We want it to express our relationship as well, so we speak to God as we would speak to a beloved and ideal parent. (It must be pointed out that some may not feel moved to speak to an actual parent in this way. Unfortunately, some parents cannot be viewed as positive reflections of God.)

What is the quality of our relationship to such a God? First, surely, is love. To offer love to God through this two-word phrase and to be ready to receive God's love in our heart—those are central intentions of the Lord's Prayer. Attentiveness is required for this, however. Along with love, we can develop confidence and trust in God. Just as children depend on their parents, we, too, will depend on God for all things as we come closer to the Lord. We will be confident that the Lord is *there* for us, far more attentive to us than we are to the Lord.

The ideal parent loves us and protects us. This does not

mean that nothing painful will ever happen to us. Indeed, in the Letter to the Hebrews, we are strongly reminded that God can be a disciplinarian precisely because he cares so profoundly for us. God protects the *essential being* that is most truly "I," the center of ourselves. God keeps our *being* safe. We *can* count on that—even through death.

Then come the words *in heaven*. In the gospels, *heaven* sometimes refers to a place or state after death, but more often it refers to our innermost heart of hearts. It affirms that God's Holy Spirit lives within each Christian and there we can know God most intimately. We can imitate Jesus' intimacy with the Father by seeking God within, where he is surely to be found.

Praying the Sacred Name

Hallowed be thy name. What does it mean to our spiritual life to "hallow" the name of God? Most superficially, it implies that God's name should not be used as an expletive. Much more than that, however, is the honor we give to the name of God. To honor someone's name is to regard it as trustworthy, reliable, the way we honor the name of the one who signs our paychecks. We trust that the signature will be valid. We act on it. Hallowing the name of God, then, means trusting God enough to act on God's promises and God's principles. It means trusting God's Word.

The name expresses the essence of the person or being. God's name *is* God in verbal form: the Word. We keep his name sacred in our heart. Then honor and respect for God himself will increase in our hearts. Soon our way of being in life and in our relationship with God will subtly change. We will appreciate God more and recognize the awesomeness of God within us. We will consult God more, seek his will more, obey him more. We will remember him—remember him in order to love him and honor him through the actions of our living.

Living in Harmony

Change of that nature will put us in touch with the kingdom of heaven within us. So we naturally then pray for the kingdom to come and God's will to be done *on earth as it is in heaven.* That means that we pray for God to be in full control over our earthly lives.

What is the chief quality of the inner kingdom? Among many lovely ones, I like to ponder *harmony*. Wherever God is trusted and followed, everything flows in perfect harmony. Our very perception will gradually change to enable us to *see* that harmony. In truth, much harmony already exists; we just miss it. The harmony of God's kingdom is experienced as an unbroken tapestry of beauty and love, where each tiny part is infinitely valuable and important, where all work together to create a splendid life.

This divine harmony is based on the will of God, the second part of this long phrase. We pray for God's kingdom, we pray for God's will, to be perfectly expressed in our earthly lives. We can't pray this honestly unless we trust God's name; we cannot accept the answer (God's will) unless we know God as our Father. The converse is also true, however. Experiencing the wonder of God's will and harmony in our life also leads to more trust and more intimacy with the Lord.

To be frank, many of us do not pray this phrase honestly. We are not so sure that we want the will of God. So to keep our integrity, we can practice praying individually, "I *want* to want the will of God." As that prayer is answered—for it certainly will be—we will gradually come to recognize that God's will always leads us closer to himself. Of course we want that.

We must be willing to do our part. We make whatever changes we can to harmonize our living with what we already know of God's will. That effort is the living of our prayer. It will intensify our love for what God wants.

Our Daily Bread

One of the most important things that God wants for us is our *daily bread*. The Greek word for *daily* is of uncertain meaning in the gospels. Like many Christians over the centuries, we may make this prayer at three levels. First, it does refer to our daily needs—food, water, warmth. It includes health, work to do, money enough to give some away. It is, in short, a prayer to receive the satisfaction of our genuine needs in this world.

Bread can also mean nourishment beyond the physical: emotional and spiritual support, food that reaches our real being and not only our body. Many things in life nourish us at these levels, and we may understand "daily bread" to mean nourishment beyond our physical well-being.

Christians have also understood *daily bread* to refer to the eucharistic bread, the body of Christ. For us, because the Eucharist is so easily available in our country, we may take this request quite for granted. Just ask a person who was imprisoned in Soviet Russia about the value of a eucharistic celebration! Perhaps when we pray to receive the food of our souls, the Eucharist, we can add in our hearts a request that we appreciate it when we do receive it.

We have deepened our trust in God; we have prayed for the kingdom of God in us and the will of God in our living; we have received all we need to live physically, emotionally, spiritually, and sacramentally. Do you sense how the Lord's Prayer begins at the most essential and gradually spreads throughout our living?

Forgive and Be Forgiven

Jesus is absolutely clear about one thing: we *cannot* receive God's forgiveness unless we fully forgive everyone who has ever wronged us. (See Matthew 6:14-15.) The slightest trace of kept resentment or nurtured grudge will prevent us from receiving the Lord's forgiveness. We pray at every Mass this exact thing: forgive me as I forgive. Is that *actually* the way we want God to treat us? Is our prayer truthful? Search your heart and find out before you say the Lord's Prayer again.

Finally, we pray to be protected from temptations and trials and to be delivered from evil in our lives or our circumstances. We all want our lives to be good, free of ugliness and sinfulness and poor choices. We don't always know how to achieve such a life, nor can we predict the challenges that tomorrow we may encounter. So we ask the Lord's protection, the Lord's help in building lives of beauty, that we may live his will and enter into intimacy with the Father, as Jesus experienced it.

An Inward Path

We know that life lived truly and well must spring from an inner condition of heart that is true and good. Our relationship to God must be sound if we want our life to be sound. That is why the prayer begins with our relationship to God.

We can grow in the reverse direction as well, however—from outward to inner. If you wish to try a fruitful experiment, think through all the above points backward. They form a kind of logical pathway, leading us from the edges of our lives back to the God-center.

So the Lord's Prayer teaches us not only to pray but also

how to live with the Lord, ever closer to God and ever closer to others whose lives reflect the same prayer. If we are using the Lord's Prayer as a pattern for deeper prayer and action, it will be vitally alive when we pray it at Mass. No more robotic words for us!

A Sign of Unity

As we know that others, too, are building their prayer on the Lord's pattern, we will feel unified with them. We can, of course, not always know if the next person in the pew is doing that. But we can, in kindly charity, assume that she or he is. Then the sign of peace becomes a sign of the unity of people whose lives reflect the reality of the Lord's Prayer.

Thus, when I shake your hand, I acknowledge that you love God and hallow his name, that you seek his kingdom and his will in your own life, that you receive your daily needs and your Eucharist from him just as I do, that we are all in the same struggle to forgive and accept forgiveness, and that none of us wants evil. What a splendid basis for unity among us! What a lovely reason to wish one another the peace of Christ to support the new life promoted by the Lord's Prayer!

These commonalities among us who go to Mass and pray heartily the Lord's Prayer cover quite a bit of our lives, don't they? Maybe if we view one another through the common elements in this prayer, we will be less inclined to complain about other's personality quirks or about community disagreements. Maybe the shared Lord's Prayer can give us a new focus for appreciating all members of our parish community.

A Month of Prayer

Here is a suggestion for your practice. Divide the Lord's Prayer into four sections. Spend a week pondering the many implications of one section. Build your prayer around that pondering. For every insight, invent a single action you can take to bring yourself more into God's life. Do it! Offer it to God. Then, on the following Sunday, *think* before you offer the sign of peace. Recall what the prayer has taught you in the past week. In that spirit, extend your hand and open your heart to your neighbor.

The next week, begin another section of the prayer. By the time you have worked all the way through the entire Lord's Prayer, your life may be transformed!

CHAPTER TEN

We Receive Holy Communion

Our experience of the Mass now nears the main purpose for which we have come: our personal receiving of the Lord in holy Communion. We have prepared ourselves for Communion by confessing our wrongs and praising our God. We have listened to God's Word in Scripture and reflected together on its meaning and application. We have recalled the wonderful history of salvation through which we always enter into the life of Christ. We have prayed for one another and offered ourselves to God as best we can. We have centered our attention on Jesus the Lord and extended his peacefulness to our family and fellow Christians.

Now we turn again to the Lord in prayer: "Lamb of God, you take away the sins of the world: have mercy on us...grant us peace."

Behold the Lamb of God

This prayer-hymn is drawn from the Gospel of John, where John the Baptist cries out, pointing to Jesus: "Behold, the Lamb of God, who takes away the sin of the world" (1:29).

The "Lamb of God" in Scripture is a symbol that synthesizes several ideas about Jesus and his mission. Let's recall the two most important ones.

First, this "Lamb" is the paschal lamb, originally killed and eaten just before the Hebrews were delivered from Egypt. The blood of this lamb was smeared on the doorposts so the angel who slew the firstborn of Egypt would "pass over" the Hebrew homes. This symbolism, then, presents Jesus as the one whose blood is shed for the saving and deliverance of his people from evil and from death.

Second, the "Lamb" is mentioned in the Suffering Servant Song of Isaiah 53. Here the main idea is that the servant of Yahweh takes upon himself the sins of the people, giving his life as an offering for their sin. He is compared to a lamb that is silent before its slaughterers, suggesting that he fully accepts the role given him by the Lord. So in our prayer, we acknowledge that the one we are about to receive is the one who delivers us from sin and evil by taking upon himself the weight of that sin in the world—and more immediately, the weight of our own sin in our own living. From this one, we beg mercy and peace.

"I Shall Be Healed"

Then, just before we receive Communion, we recall our own status before the Lord who gives himself to us: "Lord, I am not worthy to receive you, but only say the word and I shall be healed." This prayer is a paraphrase of Matthew 8:8, where it is the turning point in the story of the centurion who seeks Jesus out for the healing of his beloved servant at home. Jesus volunteers to go home with him, but the centurion doesn't need that. He understands authority, acknowledges spiritual authority in Jesus, and says, "Lord, I am not worthy to have you enter under my roof; only say the word and my servant will be healed." And, of course, the servant is healed.

Recalling its scriptural context may help us to truly pray this short prayer before Communion, which we so often mouth automatically. We are asking the Lord, in full acknowledgment of his authority and power, to heal us of our unworthiness, to make us worthy disciples by the gift of himself which we are about to receive.

In the last verse of the centurion's story, Jesus says, "...as you have believed, let it be done for you" (Matthew 8:13). Does this admonition belong to our preparation for Communion? It's worth pondering whether we actually and actively in this moment believe that Jesus will heal us and make us worthy disciples? If we do, he will. If we are on automatic—well, what do you think?

DIVINE ENERGY FOR LIFE'S TASKS

When I was a new Catholic, my experience of the Eucharist was quite intense. I couldn't get over the wonder of having this inexpressibly precious source of life to return to every day and in the midst of any circumstances. In the joy of a wedding, the loss of a funeral, the struggle with daily affairs, the pleasures of a leisurely Sunday—always there is holy Communion to give us divine energy and life for the tasks and delights of our living. Now we have come to that moment in the Mass.

We move out of our pews to receive the Lord into our body and into our deeper being. In most parishes, we wait in line and move slowly forward. The line gives us time to internalize what we have just said in prayer. It gives us time to place our attention wholly on the wonder we are about to receive.

The clarity of our experience of the Lord's presence to us

and in us will depend on the clarity of our attention to him as we approach holy Communion. Do we study the shoes in front of us? Do we think about what we are going to rush out to do after Mass? Do we fuss over the mechanics of receiving? Or do we focus on the Lord in our heart and in the Blessed Sacrament before us? Do we keep ourselves alert to him in the moment of our reception of him?

The presence of the Lord in holy Communion is the central source of a Catholic's spiritual life. It expresses and begins to effect the total interpenetration of the Lord and the Christian disciple that satisfies all our inner hungering. It is the goal we seek, the total nourishing we all need. Let's pay a little attention!

Reverence for a Sacred Action

The few moments we spend waiting in line among our brothers and sisters provides a lovely opportunity to gather ourselves in a final focus on the Lord. Here we recall for ourselves what we are doing and why we came to Mass today. Here we seek to deepen our reverence for the sacred action we will perform in just a moment: taking into ourselves the Lord of all. Here we breathe quietly, soul-deep, so that we can be wholly receptive to the unspeakable grace of this moment.

Most people today receive holy Communion in the hand while standing. Some prefer to kneel; others prefer to receive the host on their tongue. It is a personal choice. Each form has its own nuance of symbolism, of physical expression, of inner attitude.

Kneeling is probably the most powerful symbol of reverence. We kneel only before one whom we hold highest in our esteem. Most of us would kneel only before the Lord God. Standing also indicates a high degree of respect and courtesy, however, as we discussed in an earlier chapter. Standing to receive Communion, then, indicates profound respect and a consciously prayerful attitude toward the Lord.

Both open hands and an open mouth indicate an open heart, fully receptive to the active grace of the Lord in his self-giving to us. Both gestures indicate the way grace is always necessarily received: God is the one who *acts* in giving, we are the ones who *receive*.

How actively we participate in receiving may be indicated by our choice of receptive gesture. The open mouth is wholly passive, while open hands receive fully, then make a conscious action of assimilating the Lord into the self. We can choose the form of symbol that is most evocative for us. The reality—the presence of the Lord received into the disciple—remains always the same, no matter the symbolic style of receiving.

The important event, of course, occurs in the heart of the disciple who receives Communion. We come back to it again and again so that each time the Lord may give us himself. Because it is easy for our hearts to get overinvolved in other things, we lose touch with the Lord within us. By receiving Communion, we become more and more aware of his presence in our heart as we become more and more open to him there. As our spiritual or inner life with the Lord grows and develops, we also hunger more and more for him. Conscious, attentive reception of the body and blood of Christ can and does empower this movement of increasing openness.

There used to be considerable fear of receiving communion unworthily. Indeed, we do well to question ourselves about our inner state. We need not fear it, however, for we have already acknowledged that we are not worthy and asked the Lord for healing. Today, virtually everyone receives communion at every Mass. Does this sometimes mean that we are thoughtless about our inner state for receiving the Lord? Do we go forward just because it seems to be the thing to do?

Think about it. Think about it every time. It's better not to assume too much. Though I hardly think we risk divine condemnation by thoughtless reception of Communion, we do risk cheapening the greatness of the Lord's gift. This is the most sacred thing we do as Catholics. Are we awake, attentive, and full of loving gratitude? Do we hold the act totally sacred *in the moment of receiving* as we do when we try to explain it to a non-Catholic?

If we ask ourselves such questions, we may see that we are sometimes less than attentive or appreciative. If we must answer truly that this is so, then it can only help us if we do not receive Communion for a time or two, until we recover the inner attitude we truly desire.

On the other hand, many of our experiences and thoughts are acknowledged to be less than worthy of a Christian. It may be in the very midst of one of these that we most need the Lord in Communion. Can you imagine Jesus saying "no" to any needy person? After all, he served Judas, who had already made plans to turn Jesus in at the Last Supper. We can trust the Lord's compassion.

I have been told that I should not receive Communion if I was angry or depressed or conscious of wrong. It was a great relief to me to discover that when my need was conscious, Communion really helped. I found that I could not *stay* angry, for example, if I received Communion. I might still be angry when I entered the Communion line, but by the time I returned to my seat, the anger was gone. Was my reception "worthy"? Not really. But I was alert to my need of the Lord, and he healed my wrong attitude. Jesus *does* heal in Communion if we want healing, as we affirm before we approach him there.

Private Time With the Lord

After we have received Communion, we return to our seats for private prayer. What we say and do in those most holy moments is strictly between each heart and the Lord. We kneel in reverence for the Lord within, and we open our heart to him there however we wish. For some, thanksgiving is the keynote of this time. For others, it is a chance to bring every event of the past week into his presence for blessing, for healing, for release into his loving heart. For others, it is a time to ask blessings on the coming week's work and play and growth.

What you do in those moments alone with the Lord is your own choice entirely. Even the Church leaves you alone with the Lord in that time. Make good use of that prayer after Communion; it may be the most powerful time of the week for you. It completes our renewed connection with the Lord and makes it wholly conscious. It is loving, powerful help for our daily lives as we continue to include more of God in every single hour.

Have you met the Lord fully in holy Communion? If not, which part of you was absent? If you have met him, rejoice and be delighted! It is the greatest privilege of our life.

CHAPTER ELEVEN

Living the Liturgical Year

The Church has given us a great treasure. Over time, it has organized the liturgical year—the big events of Christian tradition—into a liturgical calendar. When we pay attention to it, the liturgical year becomes a spiral pathway for continued spiritual growth, rhythmic in its varied intensities but steady in its intentions.

As you already know, parts of the Mass are always the same. Other parts are variable, or "proper," according to the season or feast being celebrated. If we take the initiative, we can learn about and attend to the proper parts to help us focus on the aims of the liturgical season. Moreover, the overall pattern of the year is a wonderful support and inspiration for our spiritual life. Let's take a look at the pattern of the liturgical year. Then I strongly recommend that you get a missal and study the liturgical calendar for yourself.

A Season of Waiting

The Christian liturgical year begins on the First Sunday of Advent. Advent, which lasts approximately four weeks is, of course, a season of waiting—waiting for the birth of Jesus.

The Sunday Mass readings provide content for our waiting. They are readings of anticipation and hope and longing.

The spiritual aspects of Advent anticipate not so much the physical birth of Jesus as his birth—again and again, ever more deeply—in our own heart. In Advent, therefore, we open ourselves to more intense yearning for the Lord's presence to be newly perceptible within us.

As we prepare for his interior coming, we may undertake disciplines that increase our desire for God. Sometimes these are ascetic, a doing without. Or they may be additions—more Scripture reading, more prayer. We can choose a special practice to help us be aware of those areas in our lives where the Lord is not yet vivid. Awareness is enough in this season. We need not hurry or force changes. If we simply feel our awareness of the absence of the Lord, our desire for him will increase.

A Time to Ponder

Then Christmas day arrives, beginning often with a Christmas Eve Midnight Mass. Christmas Eve opens the whole Christmas season. It continues through the Baptism of the Lord.

If the season is to be effective for our spiritual lives, we cannot collapse on December 26 and thank God it's over! Indeed, we have barely begun to accept the interior gift that Christmas is. So the two weeks of the Christmas season is a time to ponder afresh Jesus born within us and beginning anew to work within us. Our Advent prayers will now begin to bear fruit in our experience if we are open-hearted.

If we celebrate inwardly, we can experience Jesus as freshly as we experience every new baby born into our circle of family and friends. This will not happen automatically, however, nor will it happen if we haven't pondered it and prayed for it during Advent. We cannot come skidding into church on Christmas Eve, panting from hurry, and expect to experience the Lord.

Which brings us to the problem of Advent and Christmas in our society. Likely, you need no reminder of how frenzied Advent can be. How can we focus on Advent's spiritual realities?

First, we must want to. Second, we have to be willing to make some efforts *before* Advent begins. We *can* do many of the Christmas extras ahead of time. Cards *can* be ready to mail by Thanksgiving, though you may mail them later. Many gifts *can* be purchased in the fall, and many can be mail-ordered. Not every social invitation must be accepted. Much can be simplified with a little care and effort.

Another approach, not as easy but possible, is to do all preparations as a sacrificial offering to the Lord, quite consciously making them your gift to God. Then, even if it is busy, the season is not wasted. If we take care of Advent, the Christmas season will bear great fruit, as Jesus begins to grow anew in our heart.

Widening the Circle

The feasts within the Christmas season can bring our new spiritual freshening to wider circles of our life: to the family (Feast of Holy Family) and to the community (Epiphany). The Solemnity of the Mother of God celebrates everything we have honored about Mary during Christmas.

Nourishment for New Life

After the Baptism of the Lord, Ordinary Time begins. It marks the beginning of Jesus' public work. This section of Ordinary Time lasts six to nine weeks, depending on when

Easter comes. For spiritual effort, Ordinary Time is a precious period of assimilation, of letting our renewed efforts and renewed relationship with Christ "sink in." Just as Jesus begins to teach during this season, we let our recent inner experience find expression in our daily lives.

Perhaps spiritual assimilation happens rather like digestion. We make the effort to prepare the food, we eat it with delight, and then something deeper and less obvious takes over. Certainly, it is not a time for force, though it is a good time for practicing whatever we have understood during Christmas. This practice should be peaceful, though, and light, since the season of new birth has been intense. We need to be attentive during this season so we can observe the changes that have been born during Christmas and now are growing into our being—just as we would pay attention to the needs of a new baby. We can give thanks for every hint of growth and nurture each one.

The gospel readings during Ordinary Time are most frequently the teachings and actions of Jesus. It is good food, nourishing and strengthening for the life just reborn in us. These readings give us a wealth of clues about how to assimilate and make real every day the insights and inspirations of Christmas. It is time, then, for awareness and for steadiness in practice—neither forced nor lazy—but one *conscious* step at a time.

Dying to Live Again

The next liturgical season is Lent, a forty-day period of preparation and growth. This time, we anticipate Jesus' passion, death, and resurrection.

Practically every Catholic has definite conceptions about Lent, so much has been preached and written about it. We know it's time for "penance," even though we may be a little vague about why that is. Perhaps the most common misconception is that during Lent we're supposed to do something hard so that we can then—whew!—go back to ordinary life come Easter morning.

If, however, it is our inner relationship with the Lord that interests us, Lent has a better purpose. It is a time for our own conscious, deliberate effort to cooperate in our own transformation. If our life in God is to become vital in our experience, we must be involved in ongoing and repeated transformation. It does not have to be forced, but it does have to be real. God's grace will do most of it, but our cooperation is required. During Lent we make our cooperation as conscious and disciplined as we can.

So the questions to ask ourselves as Lent begins are these: what do I want to start doing now that will bring me closer to God *and* that I want to keep doing always? If I give something up, how about something I want to give up permanently? If I undertake something new, how about something I want to do always? In both efforts, the attention and content begun in Lent will support us.

The spiritual goal of Lent, then, is to allow some dying within myself as well as remembering Jesus' historical struggles and death. Our dying almost always means the death of some self-centeredness. Sometimes it is painful, but often it is a great release into more experience of love. What can I hope to die to during this Lent? Maybe selfish habits, maybe leftover woundedness I've clung to, maybe emotional matters like self-pity or inferiority or anger.

Then, at Easter, what do you pray to be raised to when resurrected life begins? To more of God, to more of love, to more of freedom, to more of strength? Often if we are clear about what we hope Easter will bring us, we know what we need to let go of during Lent.

Holy Week, especially the Triduum of Holy Thursday,

Good Friday, and Holy Saturday's Easter Vigil is the most splendid and powerful time of the year liturgically. It can be equally powerful spiritually. To make it so, Lent needs to be intense.

You may help yourself by participating in every moment of the Holy Week celebrations (the strongest ones you can find in your area) with full attention and appreciation. The most magnificent of all, when celebrated fully, is the Easter Vigil. Don't miss it! Don't expect it to be convenient or without challenge, either. Do know that it will capsulize all your hopes for personal, spiritual resurrection in the midst of your life and support them with joy.

Season of Glorious Possibility

Easter season begins on Easter Sunday and ends with Pentecost Sunday. It celebrates the ongoing mystery that is the core of our faith and the glorious possibilities that Jesus' total self-giving opened to us. The gospels remind us of his resurrection appearances to his followers. For us, the stories bring vividly to our hearts again the reality that the Lord is alive and available.

Spiritual life can flourish with joy and fervor in the Easter season. For seven weeks, we observe and rejoice in our heart that the Lord has accepted our little dying and is actively replacing our inner deadness with his grand inner life. We open ourselves by being eager to identify with Jesus' Resurrection.

The last two great feasts of the Easter season are Ascension and Pentecost. The Ascension is described briefly in Luke 24:50-52, where we are told that as Jesus left his disciples, they experienced—imagine—joy! And they praised God. Why? Because when Jesus was no longer physically available, he became available within every devoted heart—never to leave.

It can be equally so with us, if we have appropriated the spiritual purposes of Lent, Holy Week, and the Easter Season.

Pentecost is like a seal on everything else that has happened. The risen Lord sends the Holy Spirit into the hearts of his disciples: "more" of God for them, if we can speak like that. We have received the Spirit in baptism. But it can be enlivened and reenlivened at Pentecost, if we desire it and open our hearts to it.

What is the enlivened Spirit like? It is power. It is understanding. It is peace and rejoicing. It is, most of all, an intense flow of compassion in our heart and a crescendo of love for God. It is all the "gifts" we have already heard about and a lifefull besides. All ours, if we desire them.

A Time to Stabilize

Then, without missing a step, we enter Ordinary Time again. Another time for inner assimilation and stabilization of all we have experienced and received from Ash Wednesday through Easter to Pentecost. It is a longer period because we need longer to "take in" our experience and learn to express it in our living. To help us keep going, more teachings are given in the Mass readings.

This Ordinary Time, too, includes some beautiful feasts—but space limits us to mentioning a few: Trinity Sunday, Body and Blood of Christ, Transfiguration, Assumption, Triumph of the Cross, All Saints' Day and All Souls' Day. Read about them, observe them, and celebrate them with delight in their riches!

The Spiral Continues

Then, before you know it, Advent approaches again. Are we now in the same place spiritually as we were last Advent? Not if we have chosen to live the liturgical year, to notice what is different about each season and to cooperate with its purposes. We have made a fresh start, prepared for and opened ourselves to a new birth of the Lord in us, taken it into our hearts. Then we have stretched ourselves more intently toward letting go of our self-centeredness, dying into the resurrected, eternal life of the Lord in our hearts, received all he can give in resurrection, rejoiced in his life within us, deepened and vitalized by the Easter Season. We have digested this into our hearts and lives, too, and we are different. One round of the spiritual spiral completed—and we are ready to set off on another round. One round at a time, the liturgical year will carry us into the heart of God, if we let the seasons into our own heart.

EPILOGUE

Such a short journey this has been! The riches of the Mass could fill up volumes instead of this slender book. But I hope that this walk through the Mass has whetted your appetite for more—a lot more.

If you have read this book, you are already more interested in the actual living content of the Mass than many people are. You are to be commended for that interest. It probably means you have a vital relationship with God and want it to become ever more intimate.

Knowing the Mass through and through means, of course, that it is simply too much to enjoy thoroughly every time you celebrate. But knowing the Mass well also means that it can speak more directly to your needs on any particular day. On some days we need consoling; on others, we need to share joy, on some we need to quietly steep ourselves in love, and on still others we want to shout our praises to God. No matter what our need or mood, the Mass includes something for us at every moment of life. Yet all that wonderful nourishment can go right through us and out the back door if we go to Mass *only* because we are obliged to, or if we just want to "get through it" as quickly as possible.

Once I heard of a parish that attracted many people from other parishes. When I asked what they had there, my informant said, "Well, for one thing, Father So-and-So says Mass